Indiana

interactive SCIENCE

A peony plant can grow flowers every spring for over 50 years.

PEARSON

Glenview, Illinois • Boston, Massachusetts • Chandler, Arizona • Upper Saddle River, New Jersey

You are an author!

This is your own special book to keep. You can write all of your science discoveries in your book. That is why you are an author of this book.

Print your name, school, town, and state below. Then write to tell everyone all about you.

My Picture

Name

School

Town

State

All About Me

Credits appear on pages EM21–EM22, which constitute an extension of this copyright page.

ISBN-13: 978-0-328-52090-9
ISBN-10: 0-328-52090-X
2 3 4 5 6 7 8 9 10 V011 19 18 17 16 15 14 13 12 11

On The Cover

A peony plant can grow flowers every spring for over 50 years.

Program Authors

DON BUCKLEY, M.Sc.
Information and Communications Technology Director, The School at Columbia University, New York, New York
Mr. Buckley has been at the forefront of K–12 educational technology for nearly two decades. A founder of New York City Independent School Technologists (NYCIST) and long-time chair of New York Association of Independent Schools' annual IT conference, he has taught students on two continents and created multimedia and Internet-based instructional systems for schools worldwide.

ZIPPORAH MILLER, M.A.Ed.
Associate Executive Director for Professional Programs and Conferences, National Science Teachers Association, Arlington, Virginia
Associate executive director for professional programs and conferences at NSTA, Ms. Zipporah Miller is a former K–12 science supervisor and STEM coordinator for the Prince George's County Public School District in Maryland. She is a science education consultant who has overseen curriculum development and staff training for more than 150 district science coordinators.

MICHAEL J. PADILLA, Ph.D.
Associate Dean and Director, Eugene P. Moore School of Education, Clemson University, Clemson, South Carolina
A former middle school teacher and a leader in middle school science education, Dr. Michael Padilla has served as president of the National Science Teachers Association and as a writer of the National Science Education Standards. He is professor of science education at Clemson University. As lead author of the *Science Explorer* series, Dr. Padilla has inspired the team in developing a program that promotes student inquiry and meets the needs of today's students.

KATHRYN THORNTON, Ph.D.
Professor and Associate Dean, School of Engineering and Applied Science, University of Virginia, Charlottesville, Virginia
Selected by NASA in May 1984, Dr. Kathryn Thornton is a veteran of four space flights. She has logged over 975 hours in space, including more than 21 hours of extravehicular activity. As an author on the *Scott Foresman Science* series, Dr. Thornton's enthusiasm for science has inspired teachers around the globe.

MICHAEL E. WYSESSION, Ph.D.
Associate Professor of Earth and Planetary Science, Washington University, St. Louis, Missouri
An author on more than 50 scientific publications, Dr. Wysession was awarded the prestigious Packard Foundation Fellowship and Presidential Faculty Fellowship for his research in geophysics. Dr. Wysession is an expert on Earth's inner structure and has mapped various regions of Earth using seismic tomography. He is known internationally for his work in geoscience education and outreach.

Understanding by Design® Author

GRANT WIGGINS, Ed.D.
President, Authentic Education, Hopewell, New Jersey
Dr. Wiggins is coauthor of *Understanding by Design®* (UbD), a philosophy of instructional design. UbD is a disciplined way of thinking about curriculum design, assessment, and instruction that moves teaching from content to understanding.

Planet Diary Author

JACK HANKIN
Science/Mathematics Teacher, The Hilldale School, Daly City, California
Founder, Planet Diary Web site
Mr. Hankin is the creator and writer of Planet Diary, a science current events website. Mr. Hankin is passionate about bringing science news and environmental awareness into classrooms.

Activities Author

KAREN L. OSTLUND, Ph.D.
Advisory Council, Texas Natural Science Center, College of Natural Sciences, The University of Texas at Austin
Dr. Ostlund has over 35 years of experience teaching at the elementary, middle school, and university levels. Previously Dr. Ostlund served as the Director of WINGS Online (Welcoming Interns and Novices with Guidance and Support) and the Director of the UTeach | Dell Center for New Teacher Success with the UTeach program in the College of Natural Sciences at the University of Texas at Austin. She also served as the Director of the Center for Science Education at the University of Texas at Arlington, President of the Council of Elementary Science International, and on the Board of Directors of the National Science Teachers Association. As an author of the *Scott Foresman Science* series, Dr. Ostlund was instrumental in developing inquiry activities.

ELL Consultant

JIM CUMMINS, Ph.D.
Professor and Canada Research Chair, Curriculum, Teaching and Learning Department at the University of Toronto
Dr. Cummins's research focuses on literacy development in multilingual schools and the role technology plays in learning across the curriculum. *Interactive Science* incorporates research-based principles for integrating language with the teaching of academic content based on Dr. Cummins's work.

Reviewers

Program Consultants

WILLIAM BROZO, Ph.D.
Professor of Literacy, Graduate School of Education, George Mason University, Fairfax, Virginia.
Dr. Brozo is the author of numerous articles and books on literacy development. He co-authors a column in The Reading Teacher and serves on the editorial review board of the Journal of Adolescent & Adult Literacy.

KRISTI ZENCHAK, M.S.
Biology Instructor, Oakton Community College, Des Plaines, Illinois
Kristi Zenchak helps elementary teachers incorporate science, technology, engineering, and math activities into the classroom. STEM activities that produce viable solutions to real-world problems not only motivate students but also prepare students for future STEM careers. Ms. Zenchak helps elementary teachers understand the basic science concepts, and provides STEM activities that are easy to implement in the classroom.

Content Reviewers

Paul Beale, Ph.D.
Department of Physics
University of Colorado
Boulder, Colorado

Joy Branlund, Ph.D.
Department of Earth Science
Southwestern Illinois College
Granite City, Illinois

Constance Brown, Ph.D
Atmospheric Science Program
Geography Department
Indiana University
Bloomington, Indiana

Dana Dudle, Ph.D.
Biology Department
DePauw University
Greencastle, Indiana

Rick Duhrkopf, Ph. D.
Department of Biology
Baylor University
Waco, Texas

Mark Henriksen, Ph.D.
Physics Department
University of Maryland
Baltimore, Maryland

Andrew Hirsch, Ph.D.
Department of Physics
Purdue University
W. Lafayette, Indiana

Linda L. Cronin Jones, Ph.D.
School of Teaching & Learning
University of Florida
Gainesville, Florida

T. Griffith Jones, Ph.D.
College of Education
University of Florida
Gainesville, Florida

Candace Lutzow-Felling, Ph.D.
Director of Education
State Arboretum of Virginia & Blandy Experimental Farm
Boyce VA 22620

Cortney V. Martin, Ph.D.
Virginia Polytechnic Institute
Blacksburg, Virginia

Sadredin Moosavi, Ph.D.
University of Massachusetts Dartmouth
Fairhaven, Massachusetts

Klaus Newmann, Ph.D.
Department of Geological Sciences
Ball State University
Muncie, Indiana

Scott M. Rochette, Ph.D.
Department of the Earth Sciences
SUNY College at Brockport
Brockport, New York

Karyn Rogers, Ph.D.
Department of Geological Sciences
University of Missouri
Columbia, Missouri

Laurence Rosenhein, Ph.D.
Dept. of Chemistry and Physics
Indiana State University
Terre Haute, Indiana

Sara Seager, Ph.D.
Department of Planetary Science and Physics
Massachusetts Institute of Technology
Cambridge, MA 02139

William H. Steinecker. Ph.D.
Research Scholar
Miami University
Oxford, Ohio

Paul R. Stoddard, Ph.D.
Department of Geology and Environmental Geosciences
Northern Illinois University
DeKalb, Illinois

Laurence Rosenhein, Ph. D.
Department of Chemistry
Indiana State University
Terre Haute, Indiana

Janet Vaglia, Ph. D.
Department of Biology
DePauw University
Greencastle, Indiana

Ed Zalisko, Ph.D.
Professor of Biology
Blackburn College
Carlinville, Illinois

Built especially for Indiana

Indiana *Interactive Science* covers 100% of Indiana's Academic Standards for Science without extraneous content. Built on feedback from Indiana educators, *Interactive Science* focuses on what is important to Indiana teachers and students, creating a personal, relevant, and engaging classroom experience.

Indiana K-8 Science Teacher Advisory Board

Jodi Allen
Glen Acres Elementary School
Lafayette, IN

Rick Dubbs
Monrovia Middle School
Monrovia, IN

Margaret Flack
Vincennes University
Jasper Campus
Jasper, IN

Michael Gibson
New Haven Middle School
New Haven, IN

Jill Hatcher
Spring Mill Elementary School
Indianapolis, IN

Jamie Hooten
Lincoln Elementary School
Bedford, IN

Jamil Odom
Mary Bryan Elementary School
Indianapolis, IN

Mike Robards
Franklin Community Middle School
Franklin, IN

Richard Towle
Noblesville Middle School
Noblesville, IN

K-8 National Master Teacher Board

Tricia Burke
E. F. Young Elementary School
Chicago, IL

Lisa Catandella
Brentwood UFSD
Brentwood, NY

Karen Clements
Lynch Elementary School
Winchester, MA

Emily Compton
Park Forest Middle School
Baton Rouge, LA

Pansy Cowder
Lincoln Magnet School
Plant City, FL

Georgi Delgadillo
East Valley School District
Spokane, WA

Dr. Rick Fairman
McGregor School of Education
Antioch University
Yellow Springs, OH

Joe Fescatore
Green Elementary School
La Mesa, CA

Mimi Halferty
Gorzycki Middle School
Austin, TX

Christy Herring
Prairie Trace Elementary School
Carmel, IN

Treva Jeffries
Toledo Public Schools
Toledo, OH

James Kuhl
Central Square Middle School
Central Square, NY

Dr. Patsy Latin
Caddo Public School District
Shreveport, LA

Greg Londot
Hidden Hills Elementary School
Phoenix, AZ

Stan Melby
Sheridan Road Elementary
Fort Sill, OK

Bonnie Mizell
Howard Middle School
Orlando, FL

Dr. Joel Palmer
Mesquite ISD
Mesquite, TX

Leslie Pohley
Largo Middle School
Largo, FL

Susan Pritchard
Washington Middle School
La Habra, CA

Anne Rice
Woodland Middle School
Gurnee, IL

Adrienne Sawyer
Chesapeake Public Schools
Chesapeake, VA

Richard Towle
Noblesville Middle School
Noblesville, IN

Dr. Madhu Uppal
Schaumburg School District
Schaumburg, IL

Maria Valdez
Mark Twain Elementary School
Wheeling, IL

Viv Wayne
Montgomery County Public Schools
Rockville, MD

Indiana

Chapter 1

Indiana Unit A
Science, Engineering, and Technology

The Nature of Science

This girl is collecting scientific information.

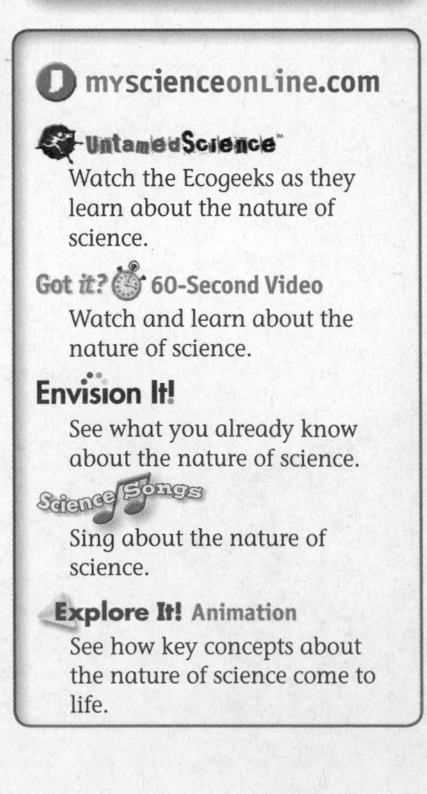

myscienceonline.com

Untamed Science
Watch the Ecogeeks as they learn about the nature of science.

Got it? 60-Second Video
Watch and learn about the nature of science.

Envision It!
See what you already know about the nature of science.

Science Songs
Sing about the nature of science.

Explore It! Animation
See how key concepts about the nature of science come to life.

Indiana

Chapter 2

The Design Process

This house for wood ducks is made of natural materials.

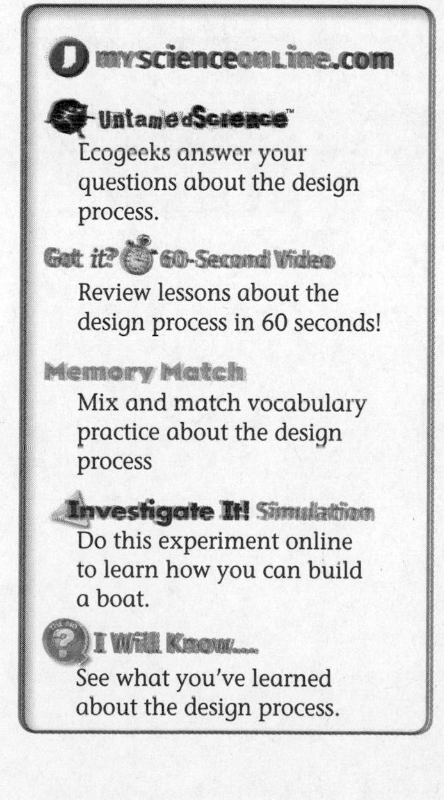

Indiana

Chapter 3

Indiana Unit B
Physical Science

Matter

Matter can be a solid, liquid, or gas.

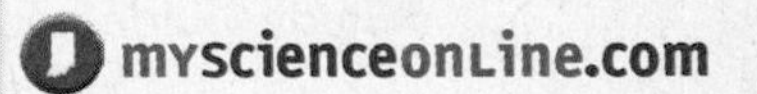

UntamedScience™
Watch the Ecogeeks in this wild video about matter.

Got it? 60-Second Video
Each matter lesson reviewed in a minute!

Explore It! Animation
Quick and easy experiments about matter.

Vocabulary Smart Cards
Mix and match matter vocabulary.

Investigate It! Virtual Lab
Find out how objects are different in this online lab.

Indiana

Chapter 4

Indiana Unit C
Earth and Space Science

Soil

Water and nutrients in soil helped these carrots grow.

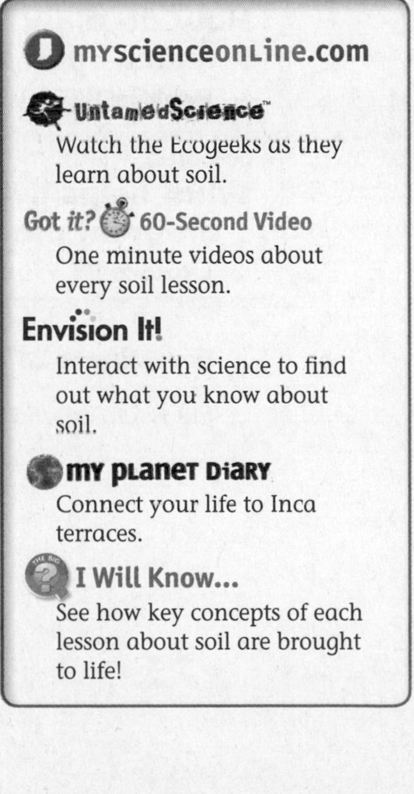

myscienceonline.com

UntamedScience™
Watch the Ecogeeks as they learn about soil.

Got it? 60-Second Video
One minute videos about every soil lesson.

Envision It!
Interact with science to find out what you know about soil.

my planet Diary
Connect your life to Inca terraces.

I Will Know...
See how key concepts of each lesson about soil are brought to life!

Indiana

Chapter 5

Indiana Unit D
Life Science

Plants, Animals, and Their Habitats

Plants and animals need each other to live.

myscienceonLine.com

Untamed Science™
Watch the Ecogeeks learn about plants, animals, and their habitats.

Got it? 60-Second Video
Take one minute to learn about plants, animals, and their habitats.

Science Songs
Listen to a catchy tune about plants, animals, and their habitats.

Explore It! Animation
Quick and easy experiments about plants, animals, and their habitats.

Investigate It! Simulation
Explore the needs of plants online!

Untamed Science™

Videos that bring Science to life!

Go to **MyScienceOnline.com** to watch exciting Untamed Science videos!

The Untamed Science team has created a unique video for every chapter in this book!

"This is your book. You can write in it!"

interactive SCIENCE

Big Question

At the start of each chapter you will see two questions—an **Engaging Question** and a **Big Question.** Just like a scientist, you will predict an answer to the Engaging Question. Each Big Question will help you start thinking about Indiana's Big Ideas of science. Look for the symbol throughout the chapter!

Indiana Chapter 5

Plants, Animals, and Their Habitats

...X on one thing a cow needs.

What do living things need?

Go to www.myscienceonline.com and click on:

UntamedScience Ecogeeks answer your questions.

Got it? 60-Second Video Review each lesson in 60 seconds!

Where does a cow get food?

136

137

Let's Read Science!

You will see a page like this toward the beginning of each chapter. It will show you how to use a reading skill that will help you understand what you read.

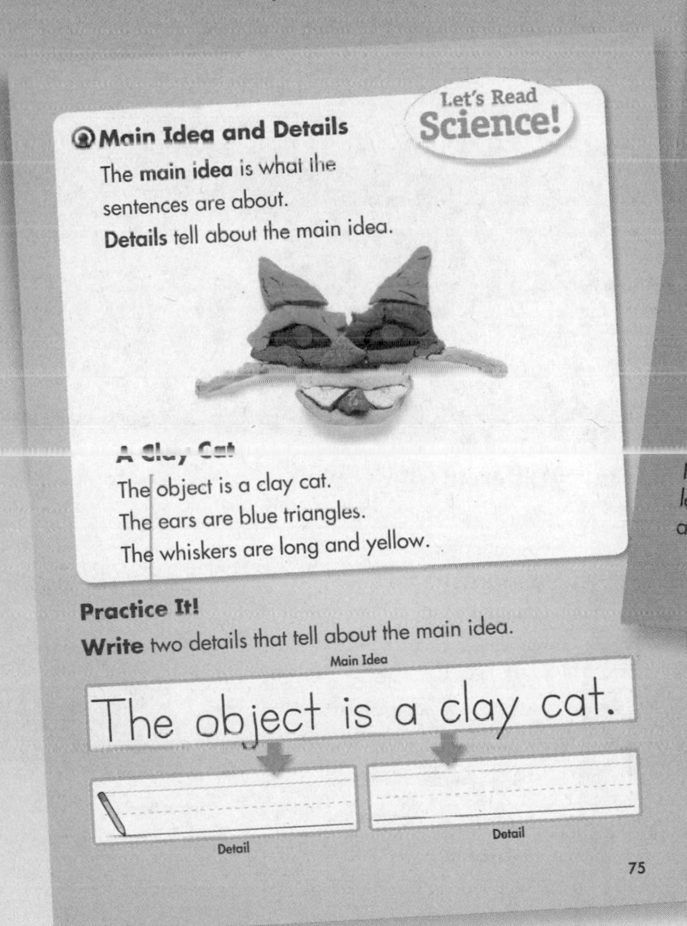

Vocabulary Smart Cards

Go to the end of the chapter and cut out your own set of **Vocabulary Smart Cards.** Draw a picture to learn the word. Play a game with a classmate to practice using the word!

myscienceonline.com | UntamedScience™

Look for **MyScienceOnline.com** technology options.
At MyScienceOnline.com you can immerse yourself in virtual environments, get extra practice, and even blog about current events in science.

"Engage with the page!"

interactive SCIENCE

At the beginning of each lesson, at the top of the page, you will see an **Envision It!** interactivity that gives you the opportunity to circle, draw, write, or respond to the Envision It! question.

Lesson 2

What are objects made of?

Envision It!

Tell three objects that people made.

I will know how to sort objects by their materials.

Word to Know

natural

my planet diary for Indiana

INVENTION!

Read Together

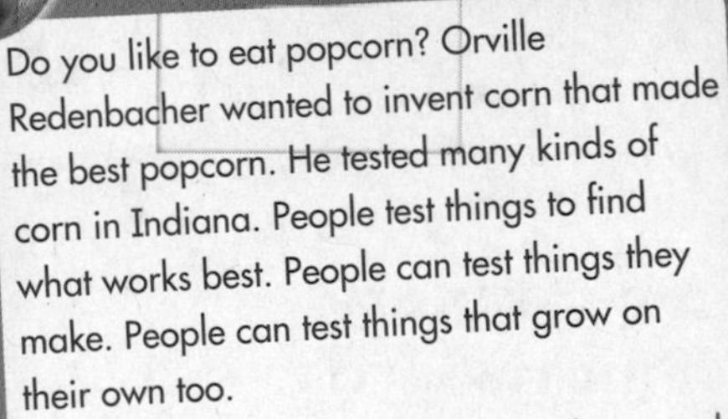

Do you like to eat popcorn? Orville Redenbacher wanted to invent corn that made the best popcorn. He tested many kinds of corn in Indiana. People test things to find what works best. People can test things they make. People can test things that grow on their own too.

Underline what Orville Redenbacher tested.

Write something you would like to test.

46

Different Materials

Objects are made of materials.
Some materials are natural.
Natural means not made by people.
Materials that come directly from Earth are natural.
Wood is natural.
Rocks and minerals are natural too.
Other materials are made by people.
People make plastic.

Write one natural material in the picture.
Write one material made by people.

47

my planet Diary

My Planet Diary interactivities will introduce you to amazing scientists, fun facts, and important discoveries in science. They will also help you to overcome common misconceptions about science concepts.

Read See DO!

After reading small chunks of information, stop to check your understanding. The visuals help teach about what you read. Answer questions, underline text, draw pictures, or label models.

Do the math!

Scientists commonly use math as a tool to help them answer science questions. You can practice skills that you are learning in math class right in your Interactive Science Student Edition!

Got it?

At the end of each chapter you will have a chance to evaluate your own progress! At this point you can stop or go on to the next lesson.

"Have fun! Be a scientist!"

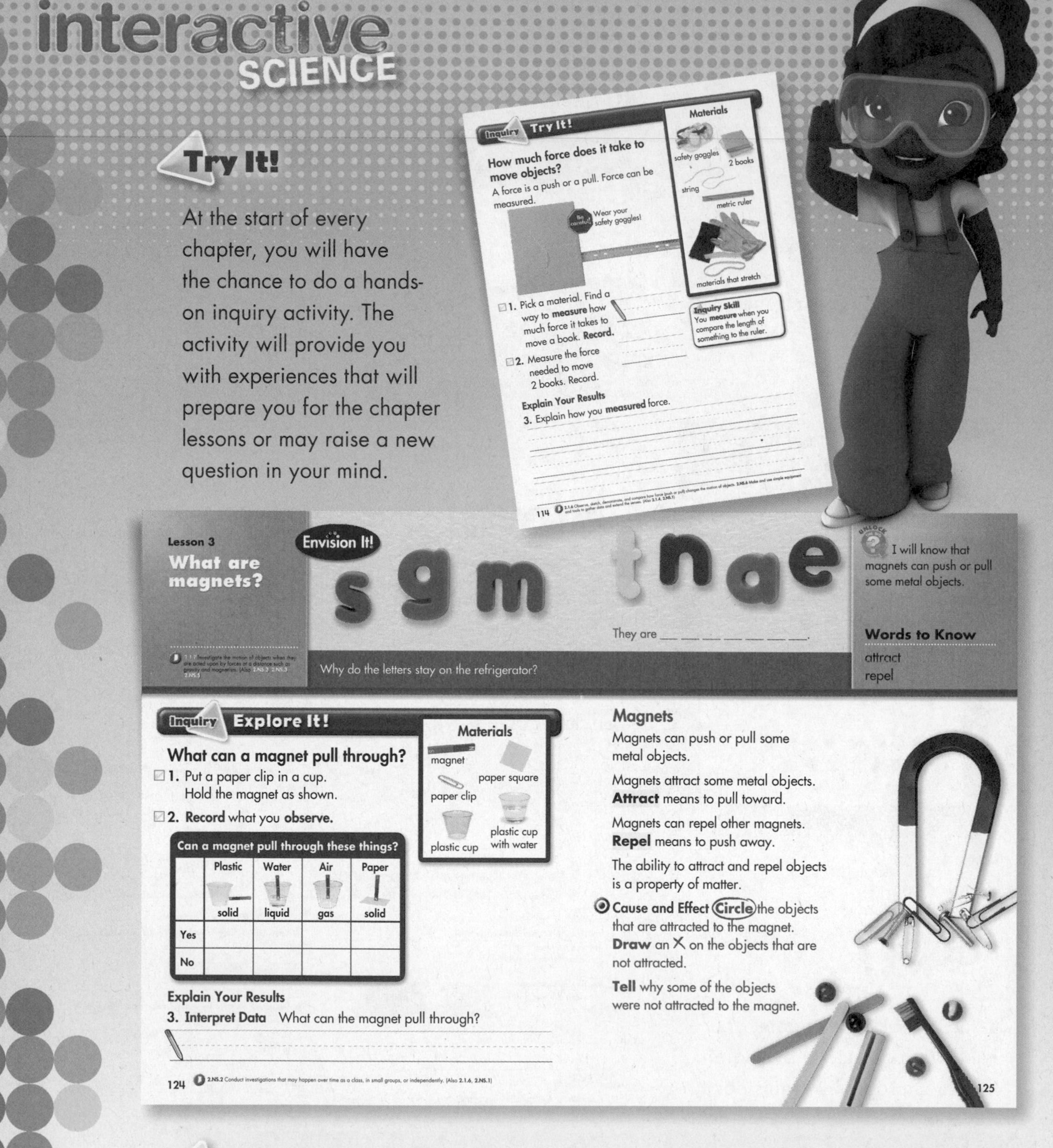

Try It!

At the start of every chapter, you will have the chance to do a hands-on inquiry activity. The activity will provide you with experiences that will prepare you for the chapter lessons or may raise a new question in your mind.

Inquiry **Try It!**

How much force does it take to move objects?

A force is a push or a pull. Force can be measured.

Be careful! Wear your safety goggles!

Materials: safety goggles, 2 books, string, metric ruler, materials that stretch

1. Pick a material. Find a way to **measure** how much force it takes to move a book. **Record.**
2. Measure the force needed to move 2 books. Record.

Inquiry Skill You **measure** when you compare the length of something to the ruler.

Explain Your Results

3. Explain how you **measured** force.

114

Lesson 3

What are magnets?

Envision It!

They are ___ ___ ___ ___ ___ ___ ___.

Why do the letters stay on the refrigerator?

I will know that magnets can push or pull some metal objects.

Words to Know

attract

repel

Inquiry **Explore It!**

What can a magnet pull through?

1. Put a paper clip in a cup. Hold the magnet as shown.
2. **Record** what you **observe.**

Materials: magnet, paper square, paper clip, plastic cup, plastic cup with water

Can a magnet pull through these things?

	Plastic (solid)	Water (liquid)	Air (gas)	Paper (solid)
Yes				
No				

Explain Your Results

3. **Interpret Data** What can the magnet pull through?

124 2.NS.2 Conduct investigations that may happen over time as a class, in small groups, or independently. (Also 2.1.6, 2.NS.1)

Magnets

Magnets can push or pull some metal objects.

Magnets attract some metal objects. **Attract** means to pull toward.

Magnets can repel other magnets. **Repel** means to push away.

The ability to attract and repel objects is a property of matter.

Cause and Effect **Circle** the objects that are attracted to the magnet. **Draw** an X on the objects that are not attracted.

Tell why some of the objects were not attracted to the magnet.

125

Explore It!

Before you start reading the lesson, **Explore It!** activities provide you with an opportunity to first explore the content!

STEM activities are found throughout core and ancillary materials.

Design It!

The **Design It!** activity has you use the engineering design process to find solutions to problems. By finding a problem and then planning, drawing, and choosing materials, you will make, test, and evaluate a solution for a real world problem. Communicate your evidence through drawings and prototypes and identify ways to make your solution better.

Inquiry **Design It!**

What do pill bugs need?

All pets need habitats. A friend gives you pet pill bugs. You must design a habitat for them. What will your pill bugs need?

Find a Problem

☐ 1. How will you meet each need?

Pill Bug Needs Chart

Need	How I will meet the need.
Air	
Shelter	
Food (energy)	
Water	

64

Plan and Draw

☐ **2.** List the steps to build the habitat.

☐ **3.** Draw your **design.**
You will use the materials on the next page.

65

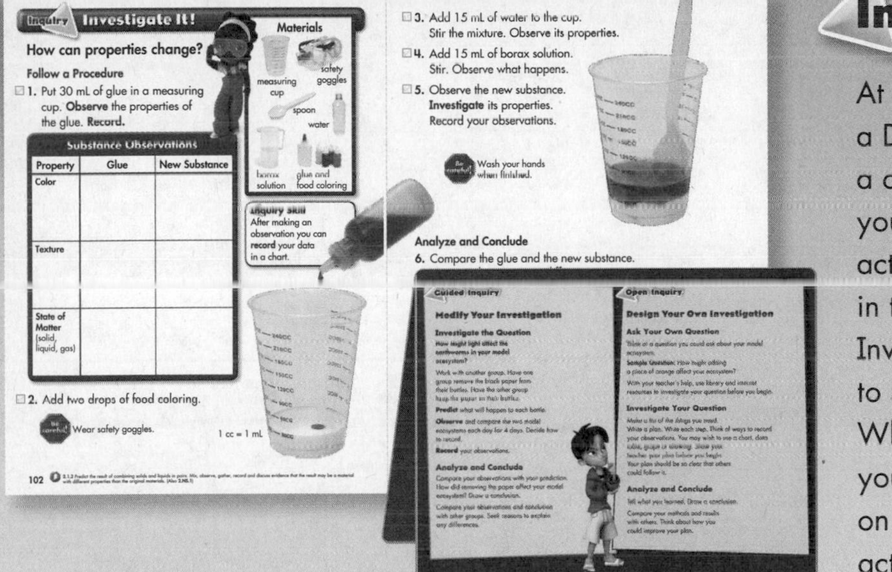

Investigate It!

At the end of every chapter, a Directed Inquiry activity gives you a chance to put together everything you've learned in the chapter. Using the activity card, apply design principles in the Guided version to Modify Your Investigation or the Open version to Develop Your Own Investigation. Whether you need a lot of support from your teacher or you're ready to explore on your own, there are fun hands-on activities that match your interests.

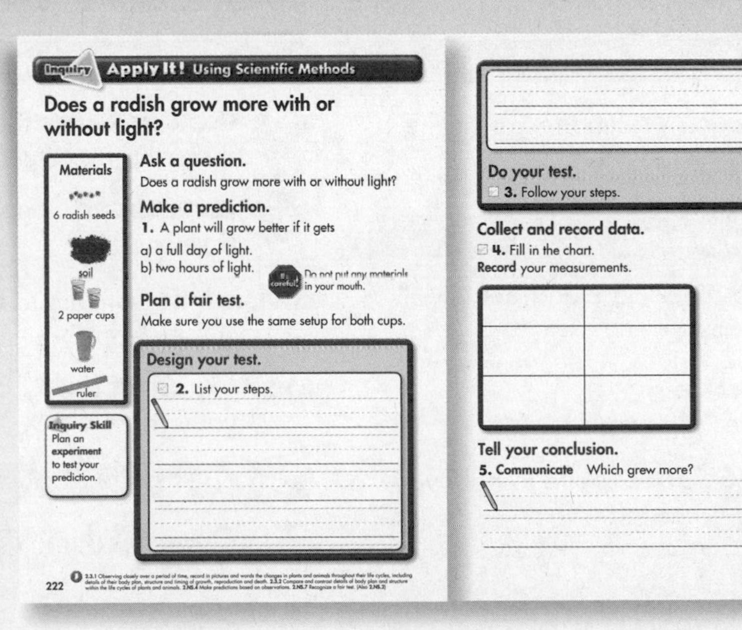

Apply It!

At the end of every unit, an Open Inquiry activity gives you a chance to explore science using scientific methods.

"Go online anytime!"

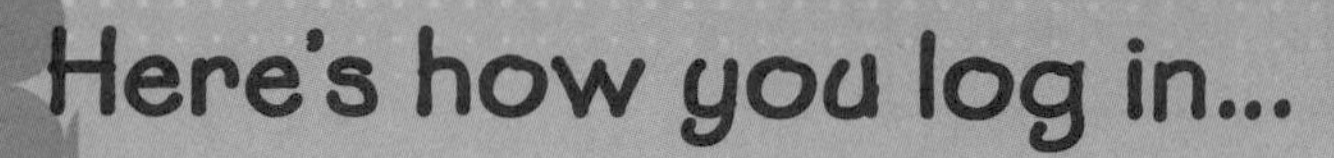

Here's how you log in...

1. Go to www.myscienceonline.com.
2. Log in with your username and password.

Username: ____________________

Password: ____________________

3. Click on your program and select your chapter.

Check it out!

Watch a Video!

Untamed Science™ Join the Ecogeeks on their video adventure.

Got it? 60-Second Video Review each lesson in 60 seconds.

Go Digital for Inquiry!

Explore It! Simulation Watch the lab online.

Investigate It! Virtual Lab Do the lab online.

Show What You Know!

Got it? Quiz Take a quick quiz and get instant feedback.

ISTEP+ Practice Prepare for the "big test."

Writing for Science Write to help you unlock the Big Question.

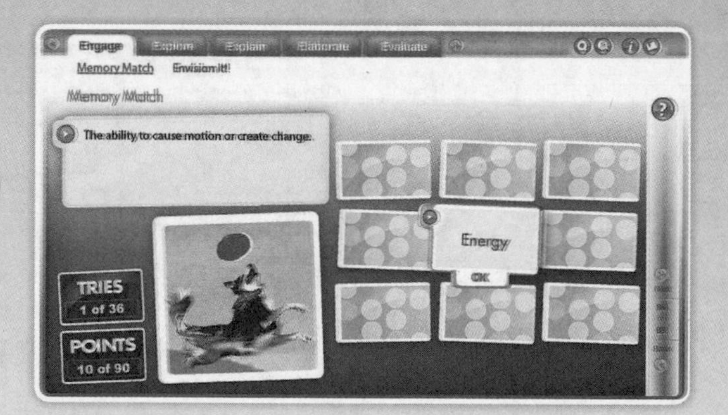

Get Excited About Science!

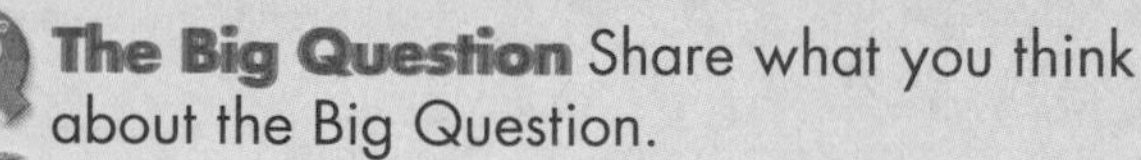

The Big Question Share what you think about the Big Question.

my planet Diary Connect to the world of science.

Envision It! Connect to what you already know before you start each lesson.

Memory Match Play a game to build your vocabulary.

Get Help!

my science coach Get help at your level.

Science, Engineering, and Technology

Chapter 1
The Nature of Science

What is science?

Chapter 2
The Design Process

How do you solve problems?

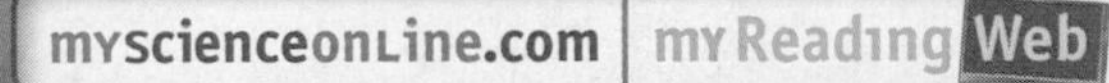

How are you a scientist when you bake?

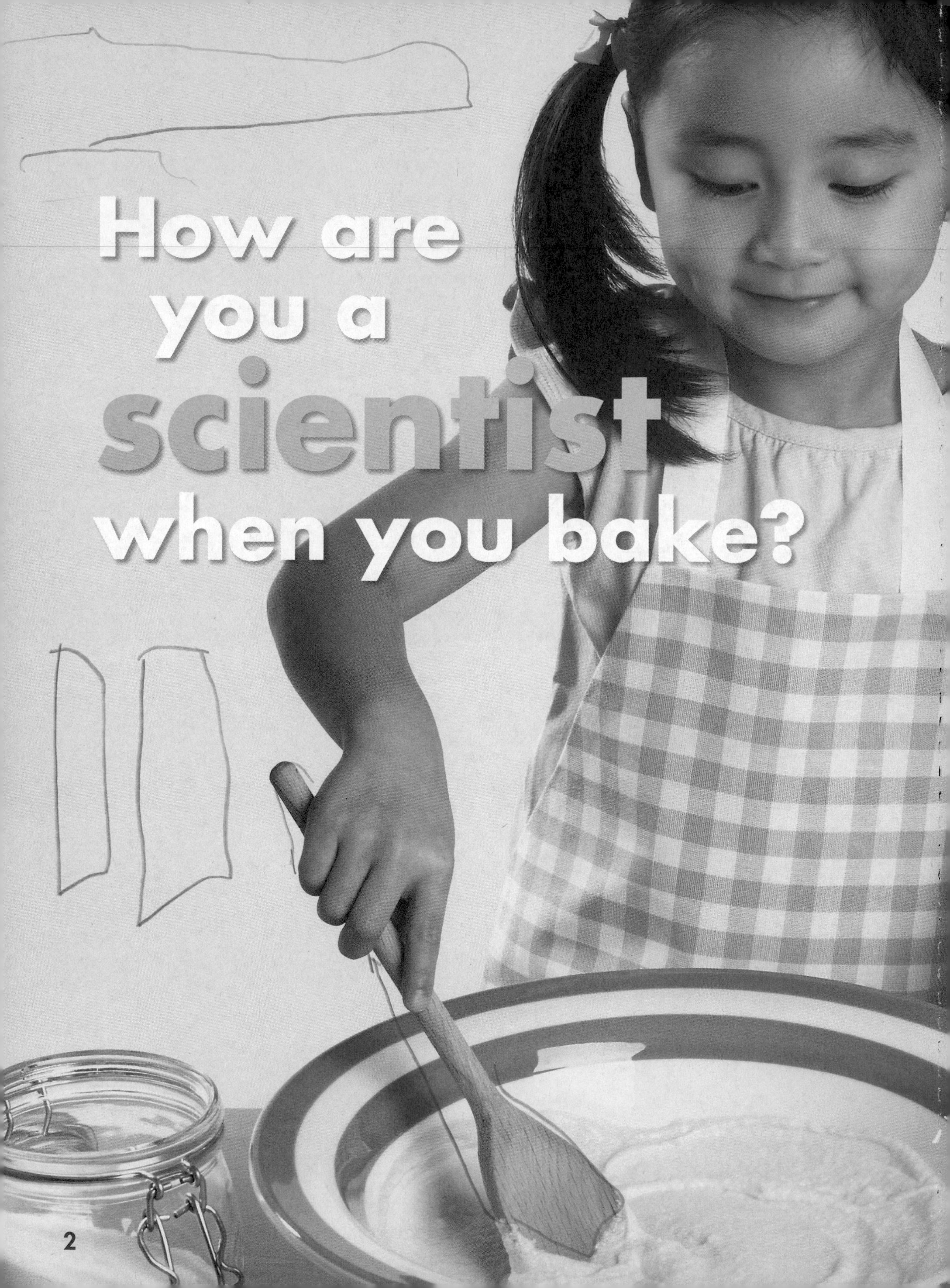

Indiana

Chapter 1

The Nature of Science

Circle a tool bakers use.

THE BIG ?

What is science?

Go to www.myscienceonline.com and click on:

UntamedScience™
Watch the Ecogeeks in this wild video.

Got it? 60-Second Video
Review each lesson in 60 seconds!

Inquiry **Try It!**

How do you use your senses to identify objects?

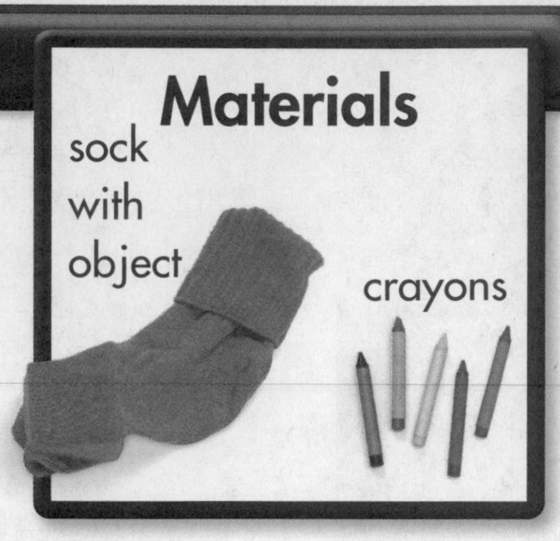

Scientists observe to find out about objects.

Inquiry Skill You can use what you observe to help you **infer.**

1. **Observe** Feel the object in the sock. Do not look!
2. **Record** what it feels like.

   p o s l

3. **Infer** Draw the object.

Explain Your Results

4. Look at the object.
   What do you see that you did not feel?

 1.NS.4 Make predictions based on observations. (Also 1.1.2)

Let's Read **Science!**

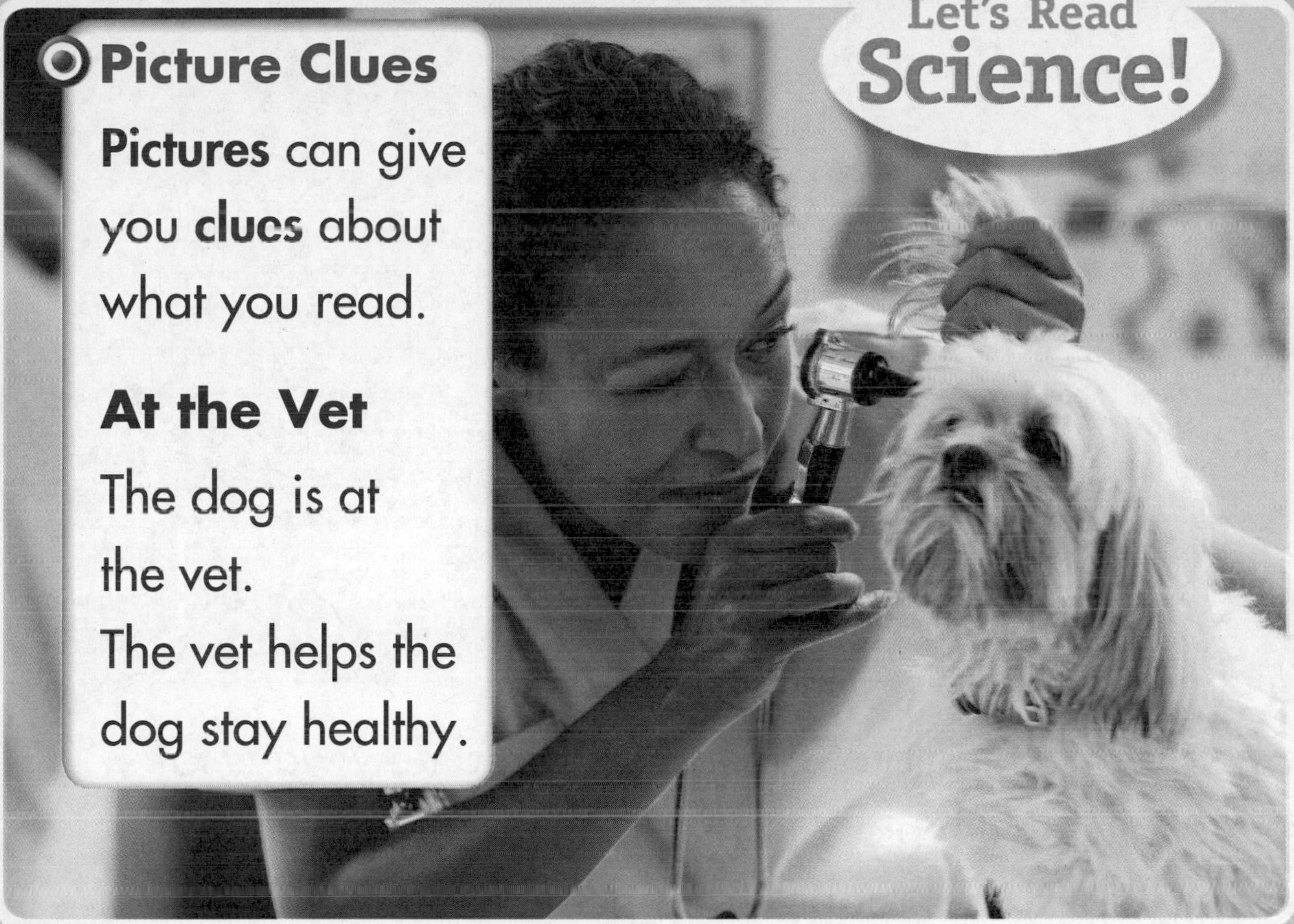

Picture Clues

Pictures can give you **clucs** about what you read.

At the Vet

The dog is at the vet.
The vet helps the dog stay healthy.

Practice It!

Look for clues in the picture. **Write** how you know the dog stays healthy.

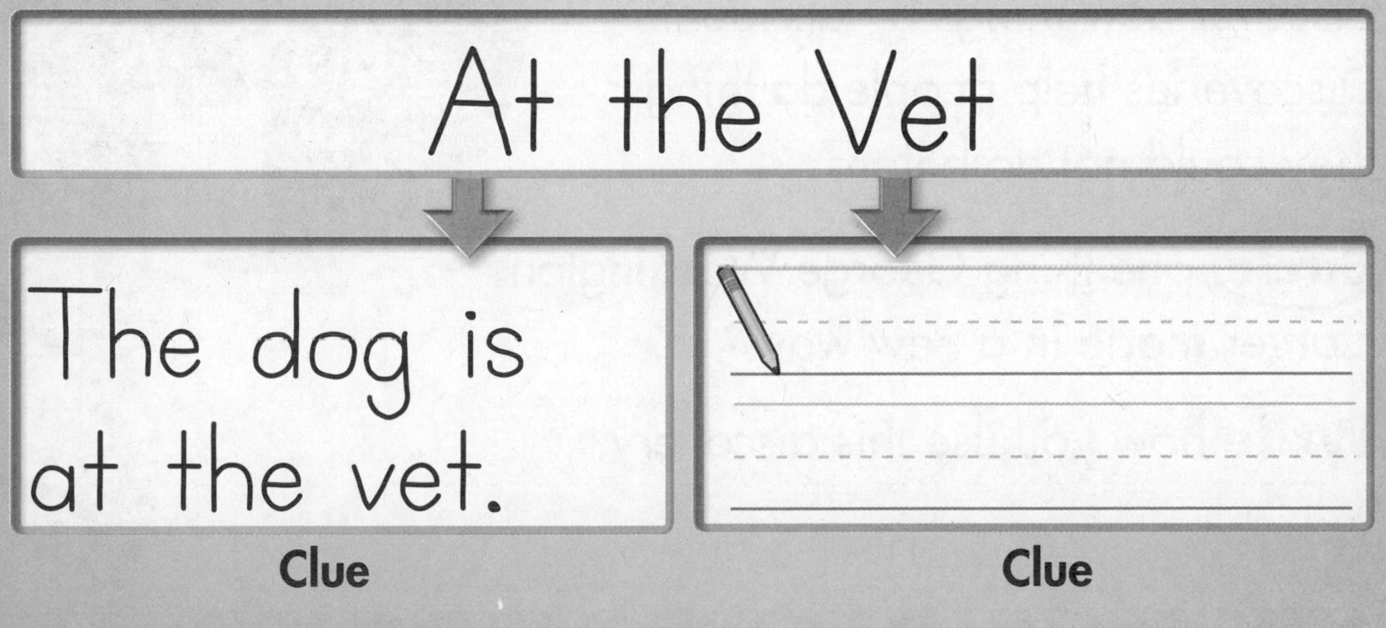

Lesson 1

What questions do scientists ask?

1.NS.2 Conduct investigations that may happen over time as a class, in small groups, or independently. 1.NS.3 Generate questions and make observations about natural processes.

Envision It!

Tell what a scientist might ask about the leaves.

my planet Diary DISCOVERY

Read Together

George Washington Carver discovered new ways to make things with plant parts. He made ink, shampoo, soap, paper, and rubber from peanuts!

Sometimes people like George Washington Carver are looking for new things. Sometimes people discover new things by accident. Discoveries help people do things they could not do before.

Circle one thing George Washington Carver made in a new way.

Write how you use this discovery.

UNLOCK THE BIG ? I will know scientists ask questions about the world.

Word to Know

inquiry

Scientists

Scientists are people who study the world around them.

Scientists ask and answer questions.

Scientists use inquiry.

Inquiry means looking for answers.

The boy is a scientist. He is studying what is in the jar.

Picture Clues **Write** two questions the boy in the picture might ask.

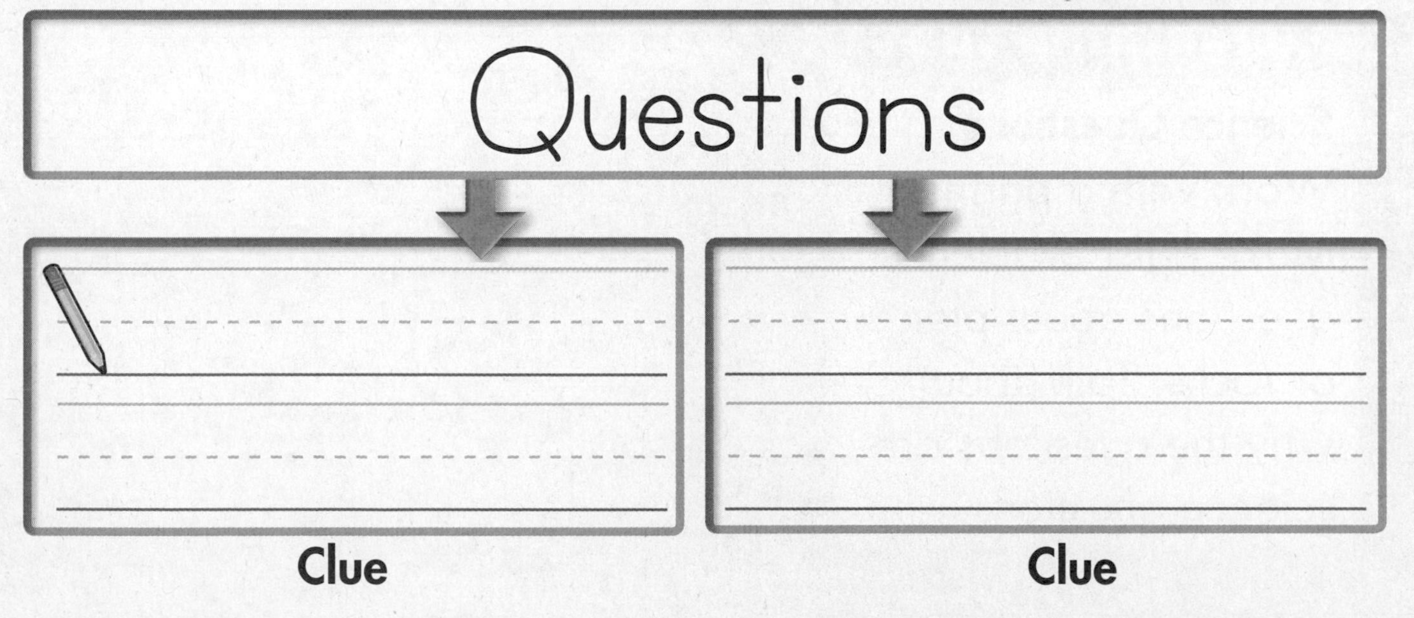

Questions

Scientists ask questions about many things.
Scientists ask questions about animals.
Scientists ask questions about plants.
Scientists ask questions about rocks and soil.
Scientists ask questions about weather too.

Write a question you might ask about this storm.

Lightning Lab

Science Questions
Work with a partner. Make a list of science questions about plants or rocks. Talk about why the questions are science questions.

Discovery

Scientists make discoveries.
A discovery is a new thing or idea.
Discoveries can change our lives.
The discovery of germs changed
the way people act.
Doctors did not always wash their hands
with soap.
People would get germs from the doctor.
Now doctors wash their hands with soap.
The soap gets rid of germs.
Their tools are washed with soap too.
Doctors do not pass germs to others.

Name one discovery. **Tell** how it
helped people.

Lesson 2

What skills do scientists use?

Envision It!

1.NS.3 Generate questions and make observations about natural processes. 1.NS.4 Make predictions based on observations.

Tell about the picture. Use your senses.

Inquiry Explore It!

How can you observe objects?

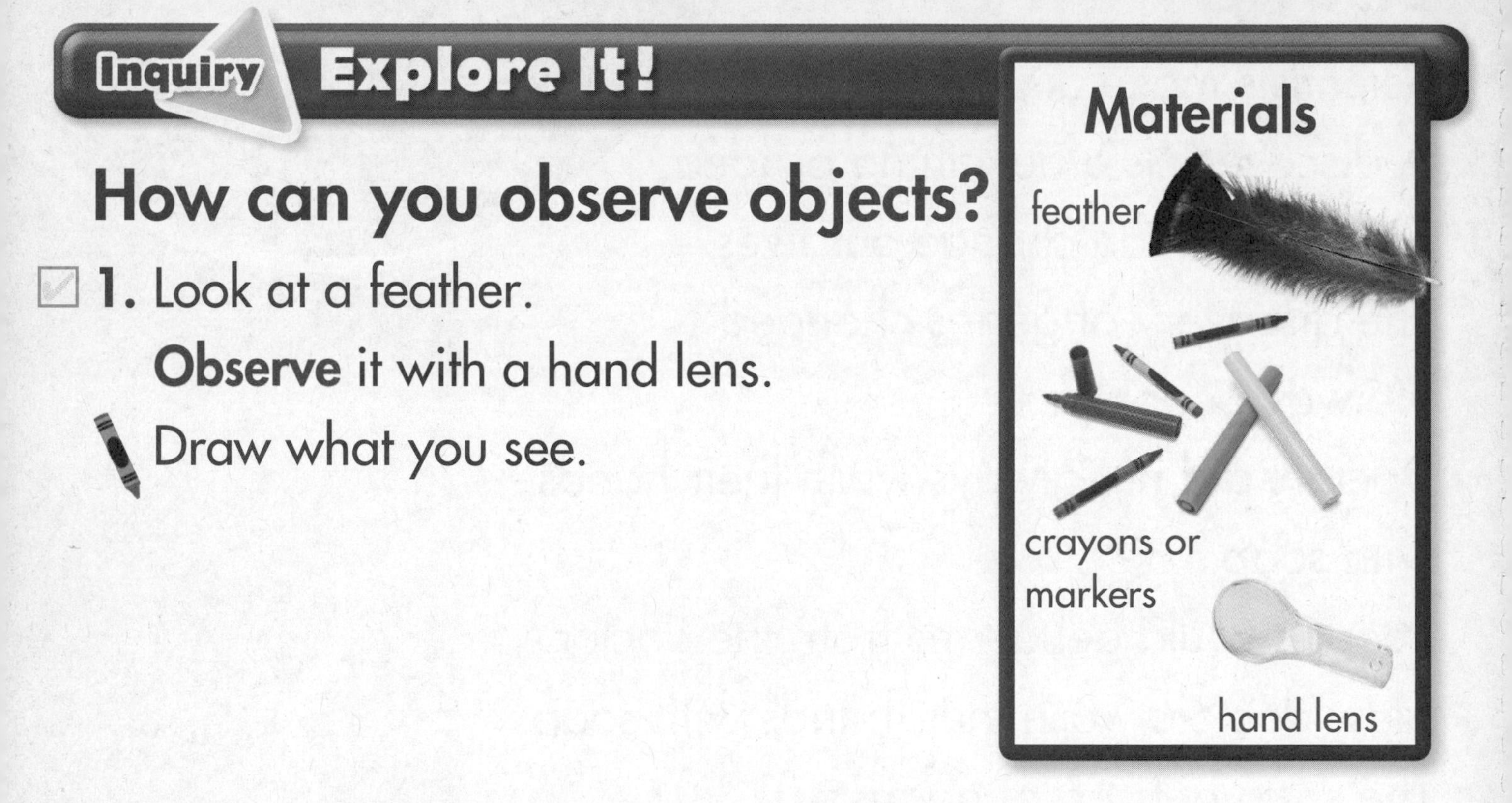

1. Look at a feather.
   Observe it with a hand lens.
   Draw what you see.

2. Feel the feather. Tell what you learn.

Explain Your Results

3. How did the hand lens help you **observe**?

1.1.1 Use all senses as appropriate to identify the component parts of objects and the materials from which they are made. **1.NS.6** Make and use simple equipment and tools to gather data and extend the senses. (Also **1.NS.1**)

UNLOCK THE BIG Q I will know skills scientists use to learn about new things.

Word to Know

observe

The Five Senses

You **observe** when you use your senses.
You have five senses.
Your senses are sight, hearing, smell, touch, and taste.
You can observe color with your sense of sight.
You can observe size and shape with your senses of sight and touch.

This tree frog lives in the rainforest.

Underline the sentence that tells how you observe.

Picture Clues **Write** one thing you observe about the frog in the picture.

Observe and Predict

You observe things.

You use what you observe to predict.

Predict means to tell what might happen next.

Suppose you observe that danger is near.

You can predict what the fish will do.

You might predict the fish will swim away.

Picture Clues Look at the fish.

Tell about their size, shape, and color.

Predict what this fish
will do when it gets hungry.

Compare and Classify

You share what you observe with others.
You compare what you observe.
You can compare how things are alike.
You also talk about how things are different.

You classify things too.
You classify when you group things by how they are alike.
You can classify the fish by color.

Tell a partner how the fish are alike.

At-Home Lab

Classify Objects
Gather 10 small objects from around your home. Observe the shape of each object. Make a chart to classify the objects by shape.

Lesson 3

How do scientists use tools?

1.NS.6 Make and use simple equipment and tools to gather data and extend the senses.

Envision It!

Tell how you can use these tools safely.

Inquiry **Explore It!**

Why do scientists use tools?

Materials

paper clips

metric ruler

1. Pick an object. Use a metric ruler to **measure** its length in centimeters. **Record.**
2. Use paper clips to measure the object. Record its length in paper clips.

Object Length

Length in centimeters	
Length in paper clips	

Explain Your Results

3. Think about the 2 ways you **measured.** Why might scientists use a metric ruler and not paper clips?

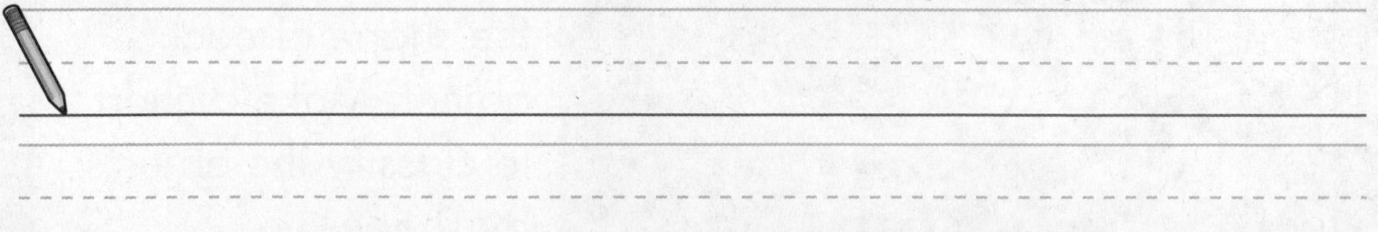

1.NS.1 Use a scientific notebook to record predictions, questions and observations about data with pictures, numbers or in words.

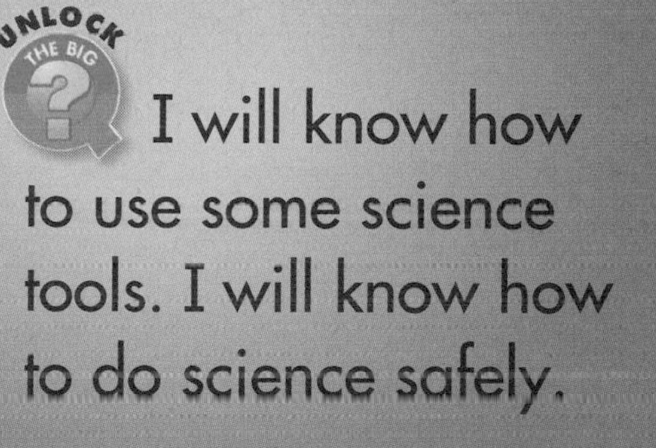

I will know how to use some science tools. I will know how to do science safely.

Words to Know

tool
safety
measure

Tools

Scientists use many different tools.

A **tool** is something that makes work easier.

You can use tools to observe.

A hand lens is a tool.

A hand lens makes objects look bigger.

A microscope makes objects look bigger too.

You can see small things with a microscope.

You cannot see these things with just your eyes.

Underline what makes work easier.

Draw an X on the tool that helps you see things you cannot see with just your eyes.

hand lens

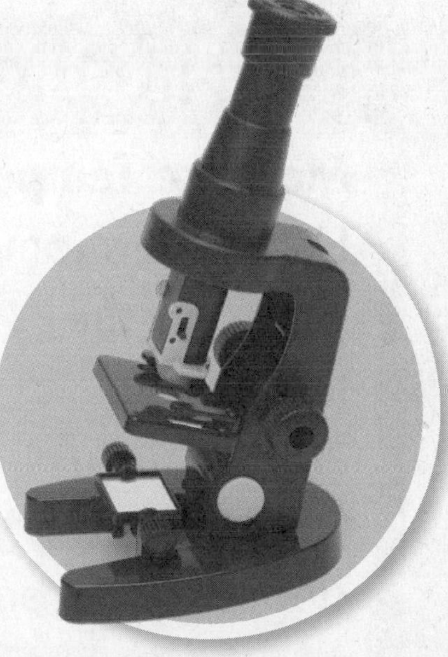

microscope

Measure with Tools

When you **measure** you learn the size or amount of something.
You use tools to measure.
Sometimes scientists do not measure.
Sometimes scientists estimate.
An estimate is a careful guess about the size or amount of something.

Circle the tool that measures how hot something is.

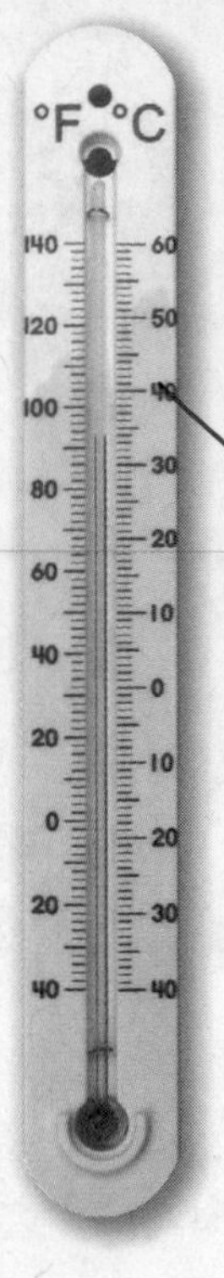

A **thermometer** measures temperature. Temperature is how hot or cold something is. This thermometer tells temperature in degrees Fahrenheit and Celsius.

A **rain gauge** measures how much rain has fallen.

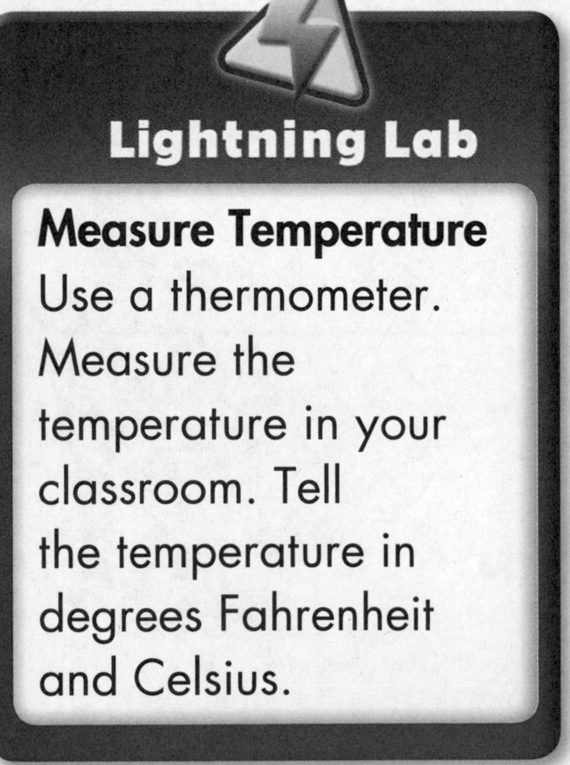

Lightning Lab

Measure Temperature
Use a thermometer. Measure the temperature in your classroom. Tell the temperature in degrees Fahrenheit and Celsius.

A **pan balance** measures how much mass an object has.

A **clock** measures time.

A **measuring cup** measures volume. Volume is how much space something takes up.

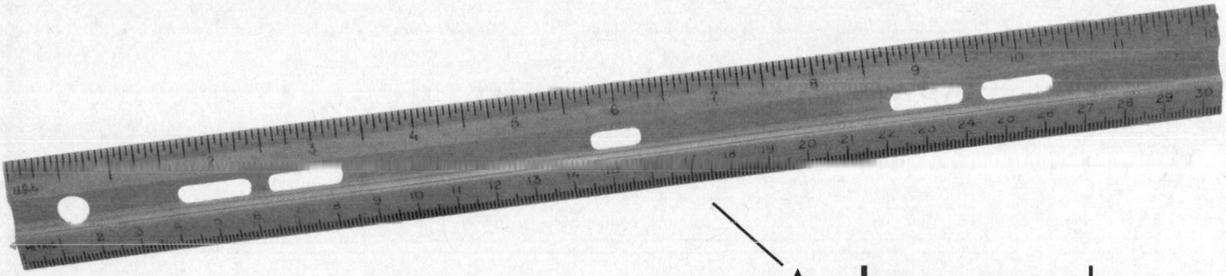

A **ruler** measures how long something is. This ruler measures in inches and centimeters.

Choose a tool to measure how long your shoe is.

Write what it measures in inches and centimeters.

Safety in Science

Safety means staying out of danger.

Follow these safety rules when you do activities.

1. Never taste or smell materials unless told to do so.
2. Keep your workplace neat and clean.
3. Tell your teacher immediately about accidents.
4. Listen to your teacher's instructions.
5. Wash your hands well after each activity.

Write another rule for the chart.

The girl washes her hands with soap and water.

Picture Clues **Tell** how the girl stays safe.

Tie your hair back if it is long.

Wear safety goggles when needed.

Wear gloves to keep your hands safe.

Handle scissors and other equipment carefully.

Clean up spills immediately.

You spill water on the floor.

Circle the rule that you should follow.

Write why it is important to follow safety rules.

Lesson 4

How do scientists find answers?

1.NS.2 Conduct investigations that may happen over time as a class, in small groups, or independently. 1.NS.7 Recognize a fair test.

Envision It!

Tell what the person might want to learn.

Inquiry Explore It!

How do scientists answer questions?

Materials

black paper

☐ Think about the following question.

Can sunlight warm an object?

Answer the question as a scientist would.

☐ **1. Observe** a piece of paper. Feel it. It is **(warm/cool).**

☐ **2.** Make a **prediction.**
The paper will get **(warm/cool)** in sunlight.

☐ **3.** Test your prediction. Put the paper in sunlight.
Wait 15 minutes. The paper got **(warm/cool)**.

Explain Your Results

4. Draw a Conclusion Can sunlight warm objects?
Tell how you know.

1.NS.1 Use a scientific notebook to record predictions, questions and observations about data with pictures, numbers or in words. 1.NS.4 Make predictions based on observations.

UNLOCK THE BIG ? I will know how scientists ask questions and find answers.

Word to Know

investigate

Science Inquiry

You ask questions when you do science.
You investigate to find answers.
To **investigate** is to look for answers to questions.

Scientific methods are a way to investigate.
Scientific methods have many steps.

Circle the word that means to look for answers to questions.

This scientist investigates plants.

Picture Clues Look at the picture.
Ask a question the scientist might ask about plants.

Scientific Methods

Ask a question.

Ask a question that you want answered.
How does sunlight change the way plants grow?

Make your hypothesis.

Tell what you think might be the answer to your question.
If a plant is moved away from sunlight, then it will grow toward the sunlight because plants need light.

Plan a fair test.

Change only one thing.
Keep everything else the same.
Move one plant away from the window.

Tell another hypothesis.

Do your test.

Test your hypothesis.

Do your test more than once.

Observe the results of your test.

See if your results are the same.

Collect and record your data.

Keep records of what you find.

Use words or drawings to help.

Draw a conclusion.

Decide if your observations match your hypothesis.

Tell what you decide.

Compare your conclusion with a partner's.

Lightning Lab

Fast Claps

How many times can you clap your hands in one minute? Plan a test with three steps. Do your test.

The boy draws a picture to keep records.

Picture Clues **Write** how sunlight changes the way plants grow.

Tell how you know.

Lesson 5

How do scientists share data?

Envision It!

1.NS.1 Use a scientific notebook to record predictions, questions and observations about data with pictures, numbers or in words. 1.NS.5 Discuss observations with peers and be able to support your conclusion with evidence.

Write what you observe about the dog.

Inquiry Explore It!

What are some ways to record and share data?

Materials

10 paper cups

1. Stack the cups as high as you can. Make a tally mark each time you add a cup.
2. **Record** the total using a number.
3. Repeat 3 more times.

Trial	Number of Cups	Total
1		
2		
3		
4		

Explain Your Results

4. Compare data with others. Tell any pattern you find.
5. You **recorded data** in 2 ways. How else could you have recorded data?

1.NS.2 Conduct investigations that may happen over time as a class, in small groups, or independently.

UNLOCK THE BIG ? I will know how scientists share the data they collect.

Words to Know

data record

Data

You collect information when you do science.
This information is called **data.**
You can use pictures and words to show what you observe.
You can use numbers too.

Picture Clues **Draw** the data that the girl in the picture might draw.

Record Data

You **record** when you write or draw what you learn.
A chart is a way to record data.

Ask five people if they like a cat, a dog, or a bird best.
Fill in a square in the chart next to the animals your classmates choose.

Favorite Animals					
cat					
dog					
bird					

At-Home Lab

Favorite Pet Name
Think of three pet names. Ask six people which name they like best. Make a chart to record their choices.

Show Data

You can use charts to show data.
You can also use graphs.
Use your data to make a picture graph.

Count the votes for each pet.
Draw one animal for each vote.

Favorite Animals

Pet					
cat					
dog					
bird					
	1	2	3	4	5

Number of votes

Write a conclusion from your data.

Inquiry **Investigate It!**

How do you know the mass of objects?

Materials

plastic cup

10 beans

balance

gram cubes

Follow a Procedure

- ☑ **1. Measure** the mass of a cup.
  First, put the cup on one side of a balance.
  Next, slowly add gram cubes to the other side.
  Then, stop when the balance is level.
  Last, **record** the mass on the chart.
- ☑ **2.** Measure the mass of 10 beans. Record.
- ☑ **3.** Measure the mass of the cup with the 10 beans inside. Record.

Inquiry Skill Scientists observe what happens and **record** their results.

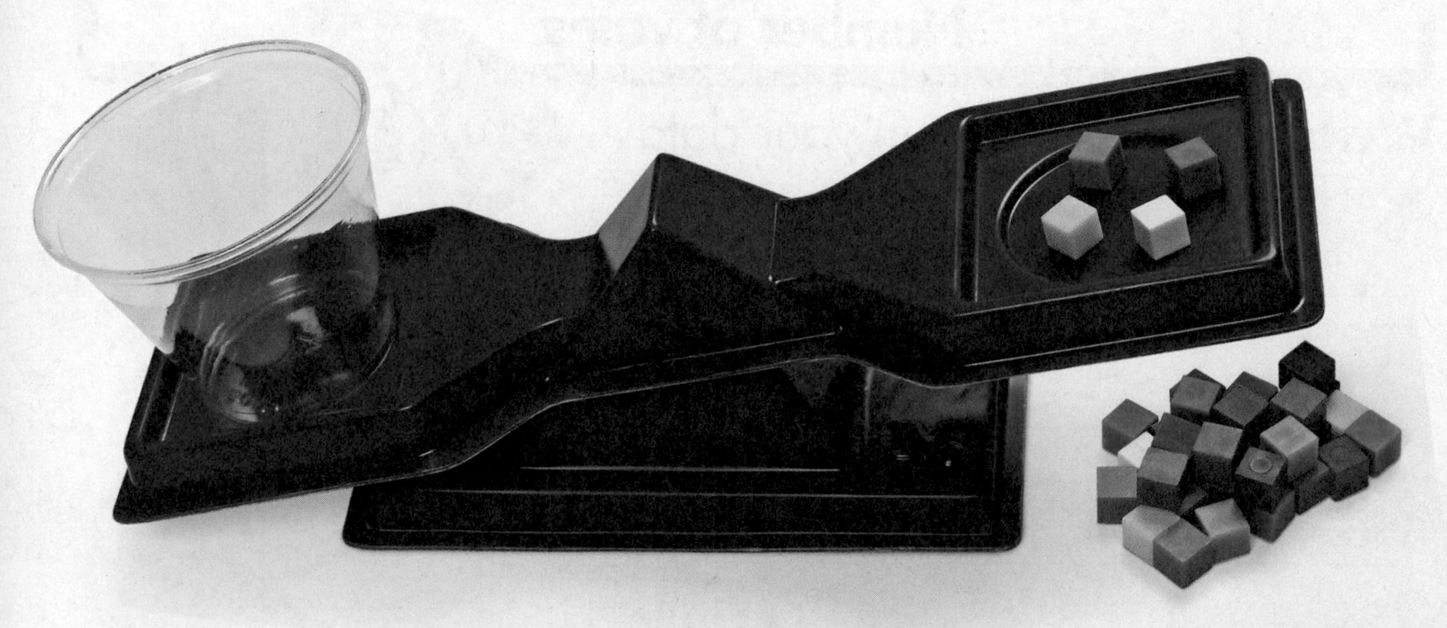

1.NS.1 Use a scientific notebook to record predictions, questions and observations about data with pictures, numbers or in words. **1.NS.6** Make and use simple equipment and tools to gather data and extend the senses.

Mass of Objects	
Object	**Mass** (grams)
Cup	
10 beans	
Cup with 10 beans	

Analyze and Conclude

4. Look at your data.
Add the mass of the cup and the beans.

_____ grams + _____ grams = _____ grams
(cup) (beans) (cup with 10 beans)

5. UNLOCK THE BIG Q **Draw a Conclusion** Did the cup and beans have the same mass together as they did separately?

Meteorologist

1.NS.1, 1.NS.5, 1.NS.6

Dr. J. Marshall Shepherd spent many years as a research meteorologist at NASA. He now teaches about weather.

A meteorologist is a scientist who studies or predicts the weather. Some meteorologists use special weather tools to collect data.

Some meteorologists make special maps about the weather. Meteorologists share their predictions about what the weather will be like.

Picture Clues Look at the picture of Dr. Shepherd working. **Write** what tools he uses to study the weather.

Vocabulary Smart Cards

inquiry
observe
tool
measure
safety
investigate
data
record

Play a Game!

Cut out the cards.

Work with a partner.

Pick a card.

Act out the word.

Have your partner guess the word.

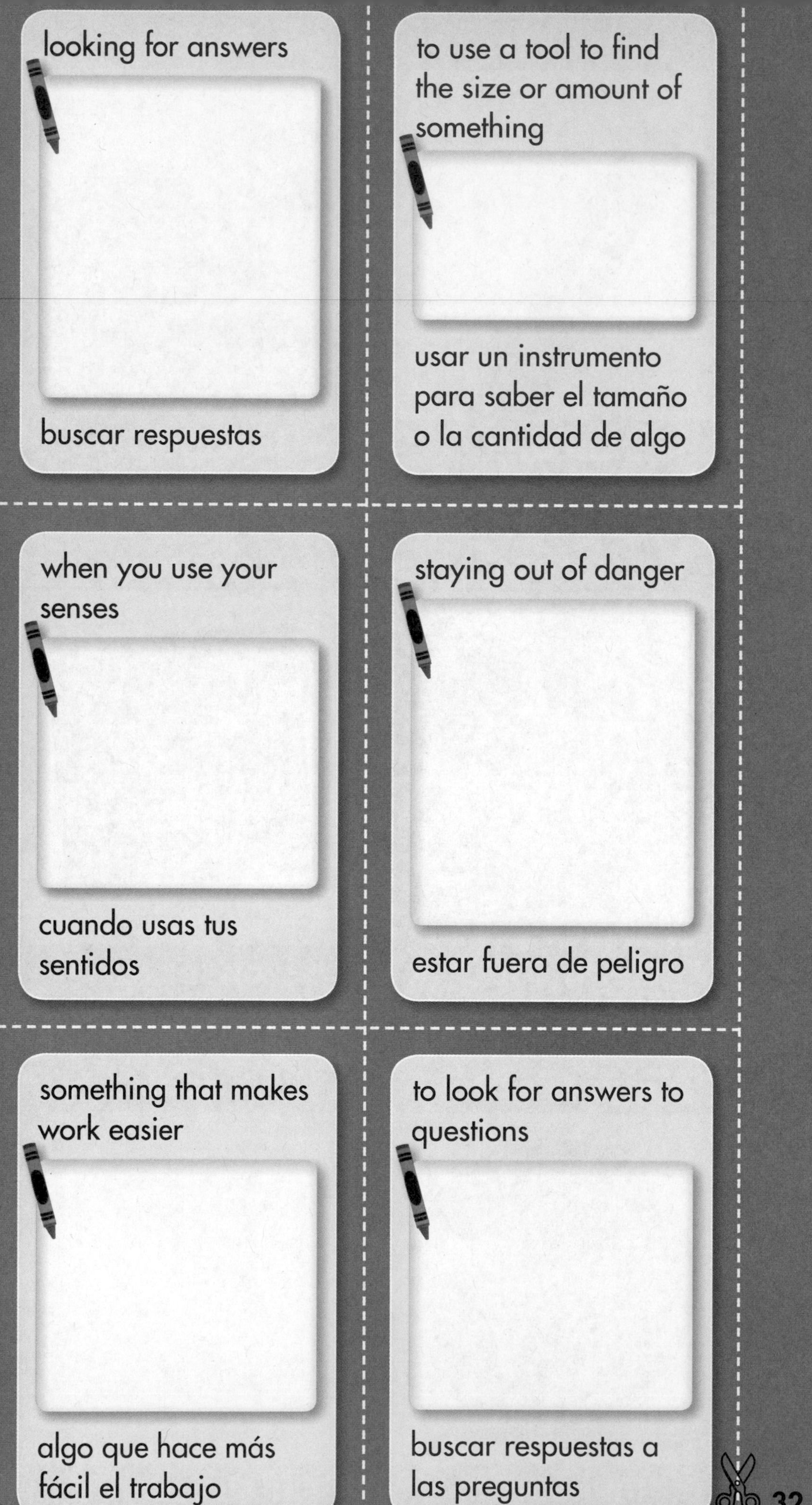

looking for answers
buscar respuestas
to use a tool to find the size or amount of something
usar un instrumento para saber el tamaño o la cantidad de algo
when you use your senses
cuando usas tus sentidos
staying out of danger
estar fuera de peligro
something that makes work easier
algo que hace más fácil el trabajo
to look for answers to questions
buscar respuestas a las preguntas

data
datos
record
Favorite Animals
cat
dog
bird
registrar

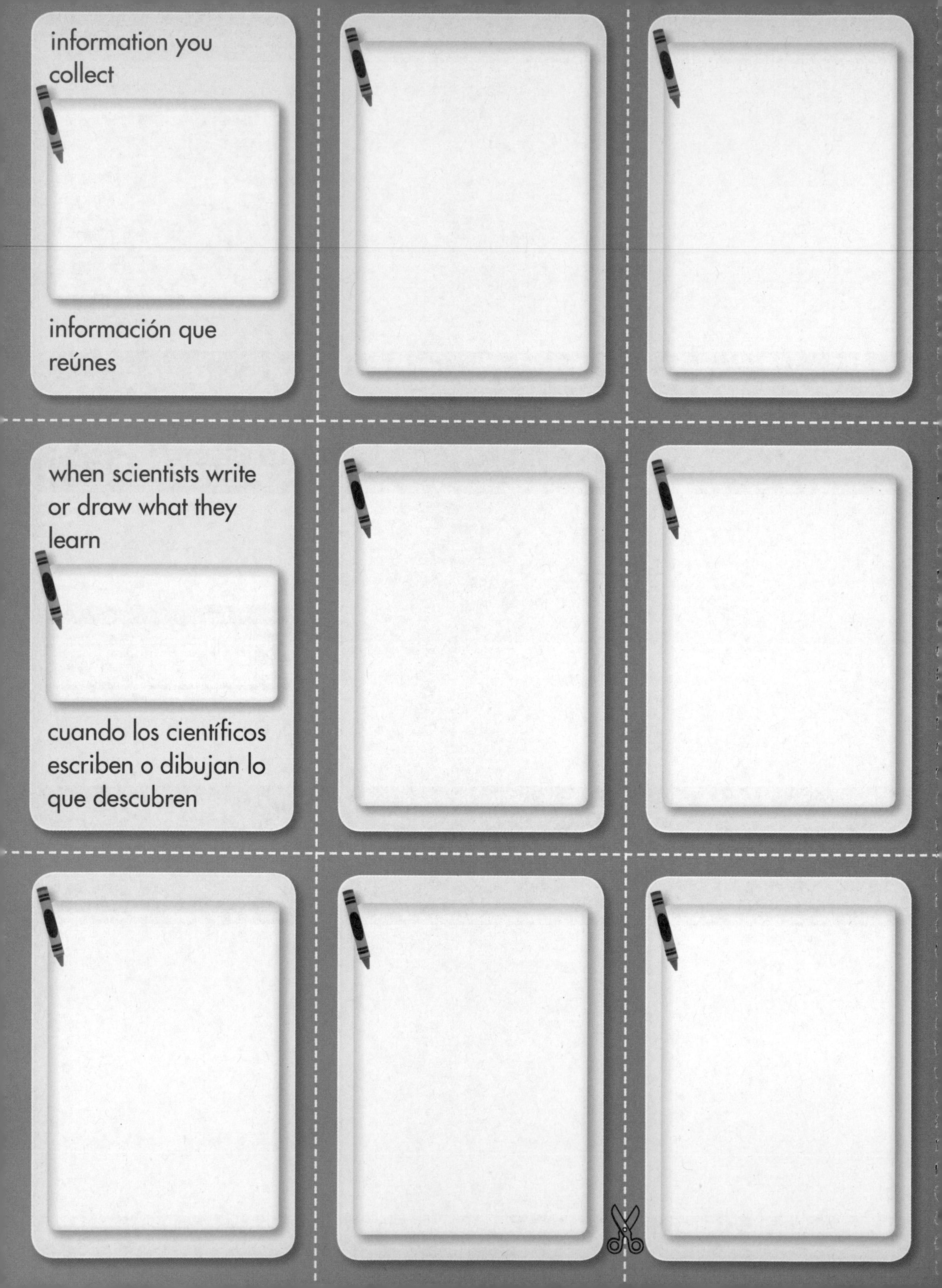
information you collect
información que reúnes
when scientists write or draw what they learn
cuando los científicos escriben o dibujan lo que descubren

Record and Share

You decide how well your solution works.

You plan again to make your solution better.

Next, you record your new plan.

You write and draw.

You use labels.

A **label** shows what something is.

This helps you remember what you learn.

You can use your solution again.

Last, you can show others your solution. You can tell how your solution meets your goal.

Label the house for wood ducks.

Sequence **Tell** the sequence you can use to build a house for wood ducks. Use the words first, next, and last.

Inquiry **Investigate It!**

How can you build a boat?

In this activity you will build a **model** of a boat using foil.

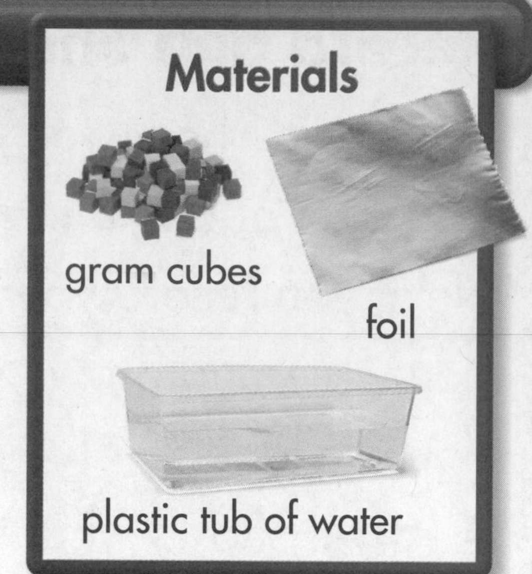

Inquiry Skill
When you **predict,** you tell what you think might happen.

Follow a Procedure

☑ **1. Design** a boat that will float.
Draw your design.

☑ **2.** Build your boat. Test it in the tub of water.

1.DP.3 Document the design throughout the entire design process. **1.DP.6**. Create the solution. **1.DP.8**. Communicate the solution with drawings or prototypes. **1.DP.9**. Communicate how to improve the solution. (Also **1.DP.4**, **1.DP.7**)

☑ **3.** Add gram cubes to your boat until it sinks. **Record.**

☑ **4.** **Redesign** your boat to hold more cubes. **Predict** how many gram cubes it will hold before it sinks. Record.

☑ **5.** Test your prediction. Add cubes to your boat until it sinks. Record.

Analyze and Conclude

6. Draw a Conclusion Did your boat hold more or less cubes than your **prediction**?

7. How did you **redesign** your boat to hold more gram cubes?

Go Green!

Solar Power

1.DP.2

You use electricity every day. Electricity is made in many ways. Using coal to make electricity makes pollution. This pollution needs to be cleaned up.

Scientists study solar power technology. Solar power uses energy from the sun to make electricity. Energy from the sun makes much less pollution than coal.

Write how you can use less electricity.

Some traffic lights use solar power.

Vocabulary Smart Cards

technology
natural
goal
solution
label

Cut out the cards.

Work with a partner.

Pick a card.

Show your partner the front of the card.

Have your partner tell what the word means.

solution

solución

technology

tecnología

label

rótulo

natural

natural

goal

objetivo

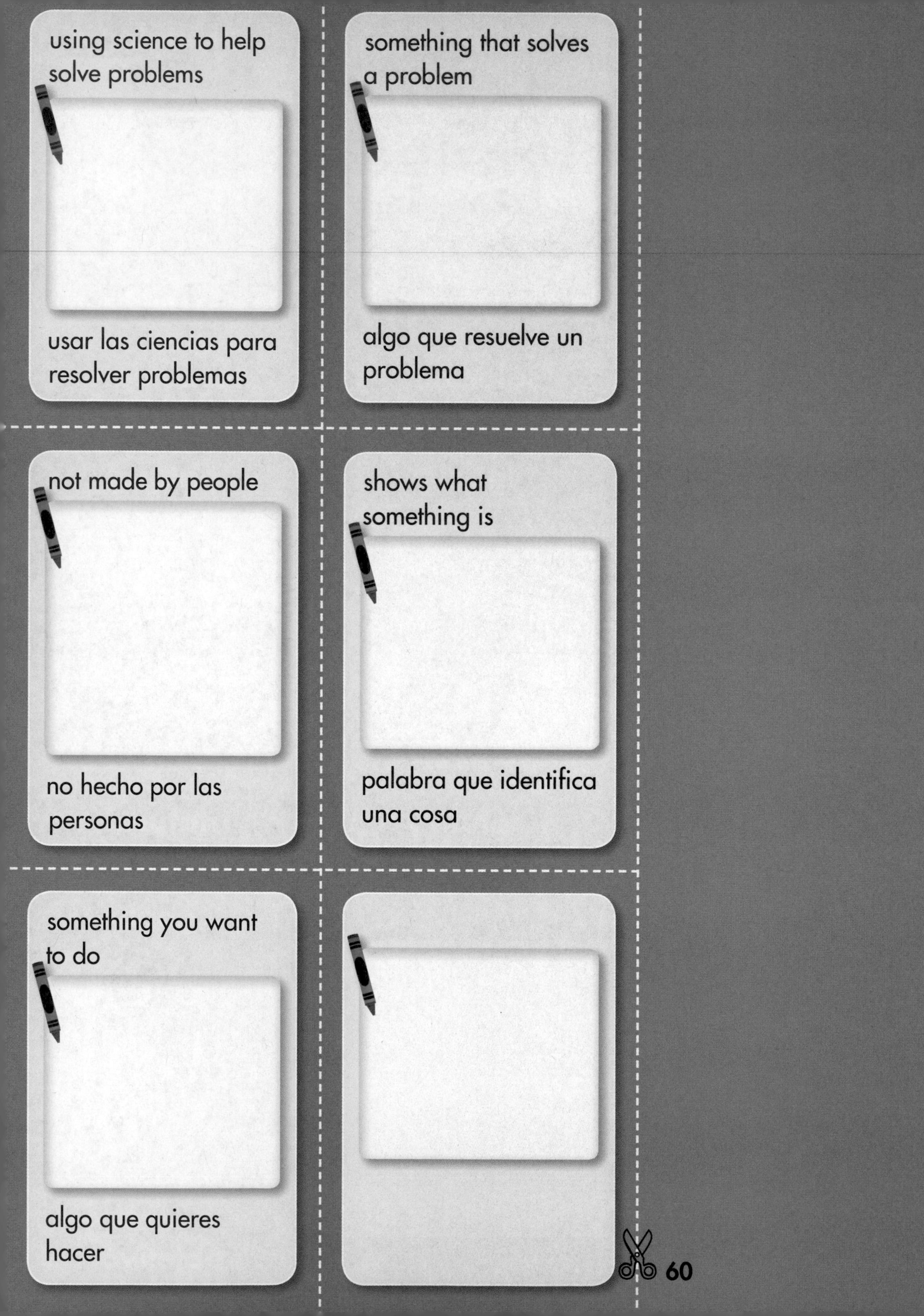
using science to help solve problems
usar las ciencias para resolver problemas
something that solves a problem
algo que resuelve un problema
not made by people
no hecho por las personas
shows what something is
palabra que identifica una cosa
something you want to do
algo que quieres hacer

Study Guide

REVIEW THE BIG ? How do you solve problems?

Lesson 1

What is technology?

- Technology is any tool that helps people.
- People use technology to solve problems.

Lesson 2

What are objects made of?

- Materials not made by people are natural.
- You can sort objects by their materials.

Lesson 3

What is the design process?

- Something you want to do is a goal.
- You can record your solution with labels.

Chapter Review

How do you solve problems?

Lesson 1

1.DP.1, 1.DP.2, 1.DP.4

1. Vocabulary Put an X on a kind of technology.

2. Apply Technology helps solve problems. **Write** a problem you would like to solve.

Lesson 2

1.4.1

3. Sort Circle the object with no natural materials.

4. Describe **Write** an object that has natural materials and materials made by people.

Lesson 3

1.DP.7, 1.DP.8, 1.4.3

5. Sequence **Write** what you do first to solve a problem.

6. How could you test a new ant farm? **Circle** the letter.

A. put food inside
B. tell about the ant farm
C. draw the ant farm
D. see if ants will live there

Got it?

Stop! I need help with

Go! Now I know

Inquiry **Design It!**

What do pill bugs need?

All pets need habitats. A friend gives you pet pill bugs. You must design a habitat for them. What will your pill bugs need?

Find a Problem

☑ **1.** How will you meet each need?

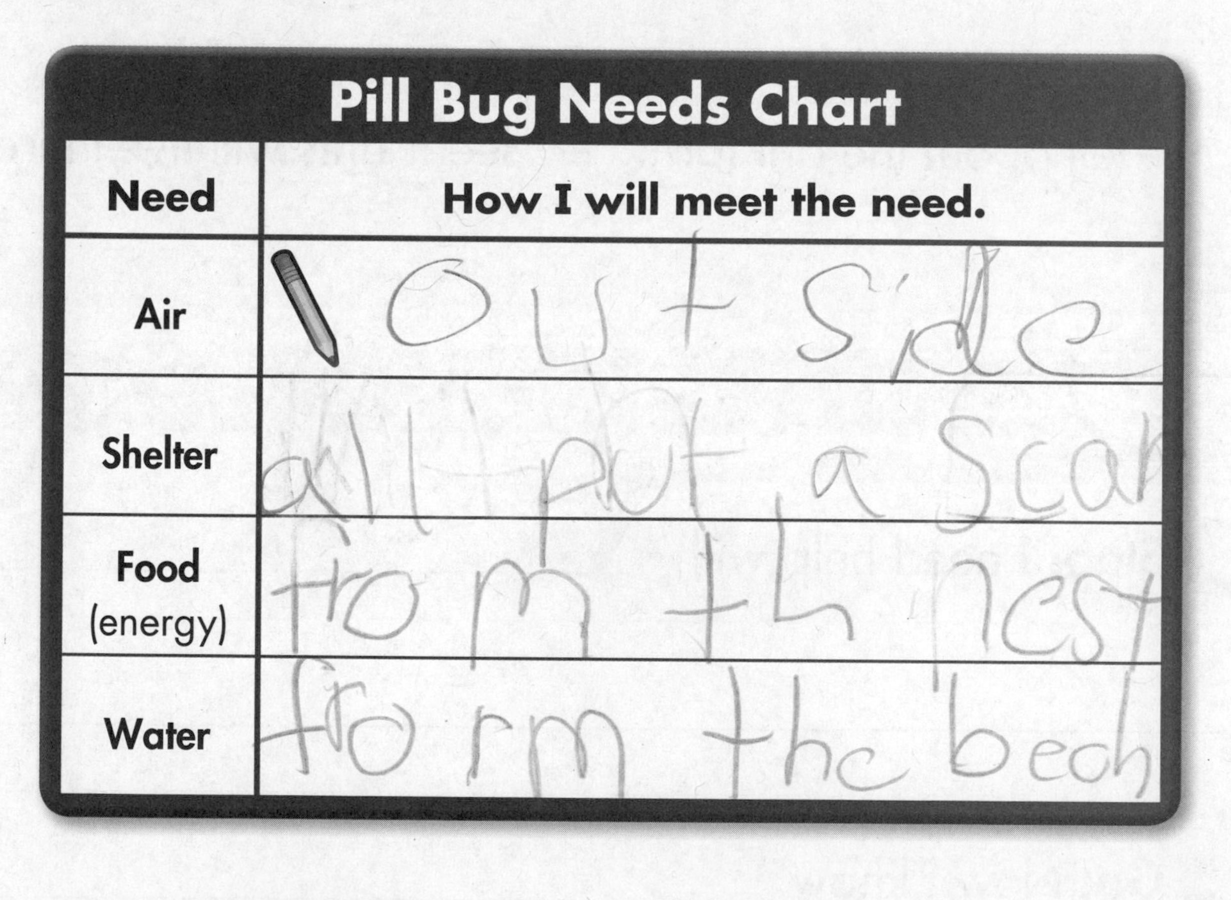

Pill Bug Needs Chart

Need	How I will meet the need.
Air	outside
Shelter	all put a scar
Food (energy)	from th nest
Water	frorm the bech

Plan and Draw

2. List the steps to build the habitat.

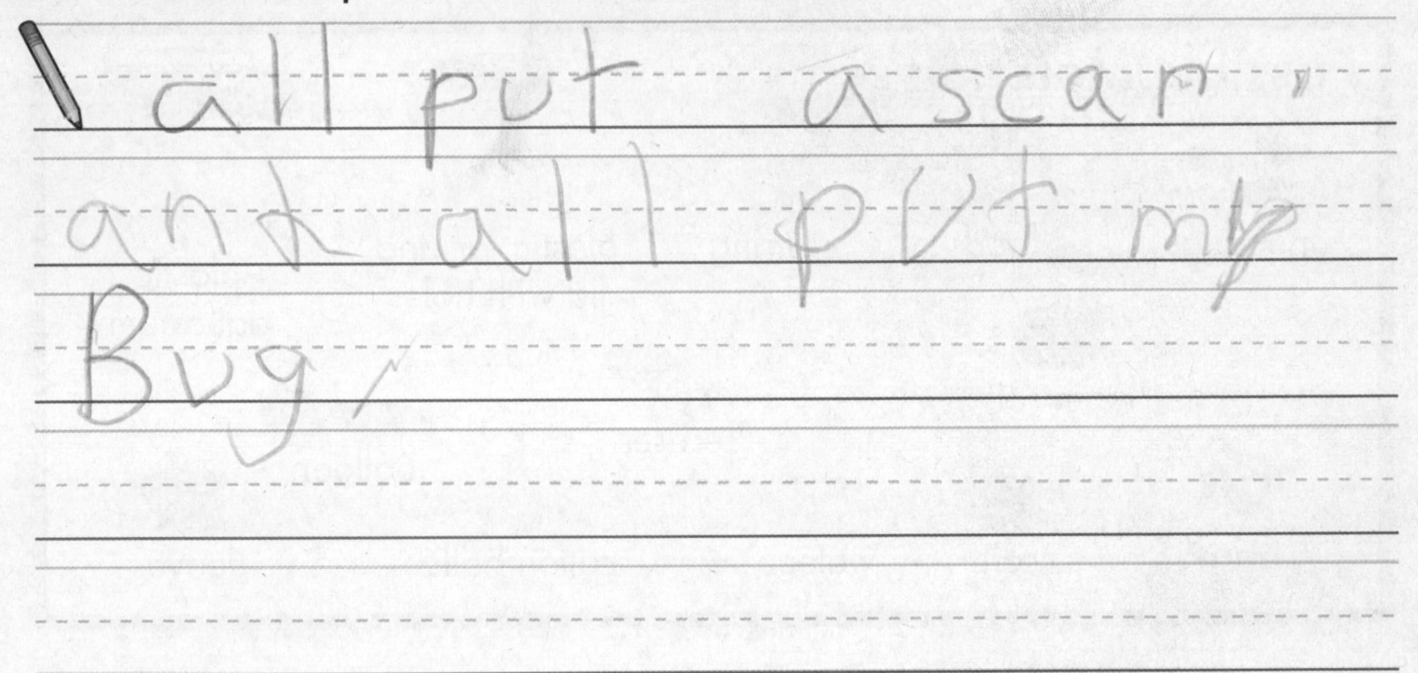

3. Draw your **design.**
You will use the materials on the next page.

Choose Materials

☑ **4.** Circle the materials you will use.

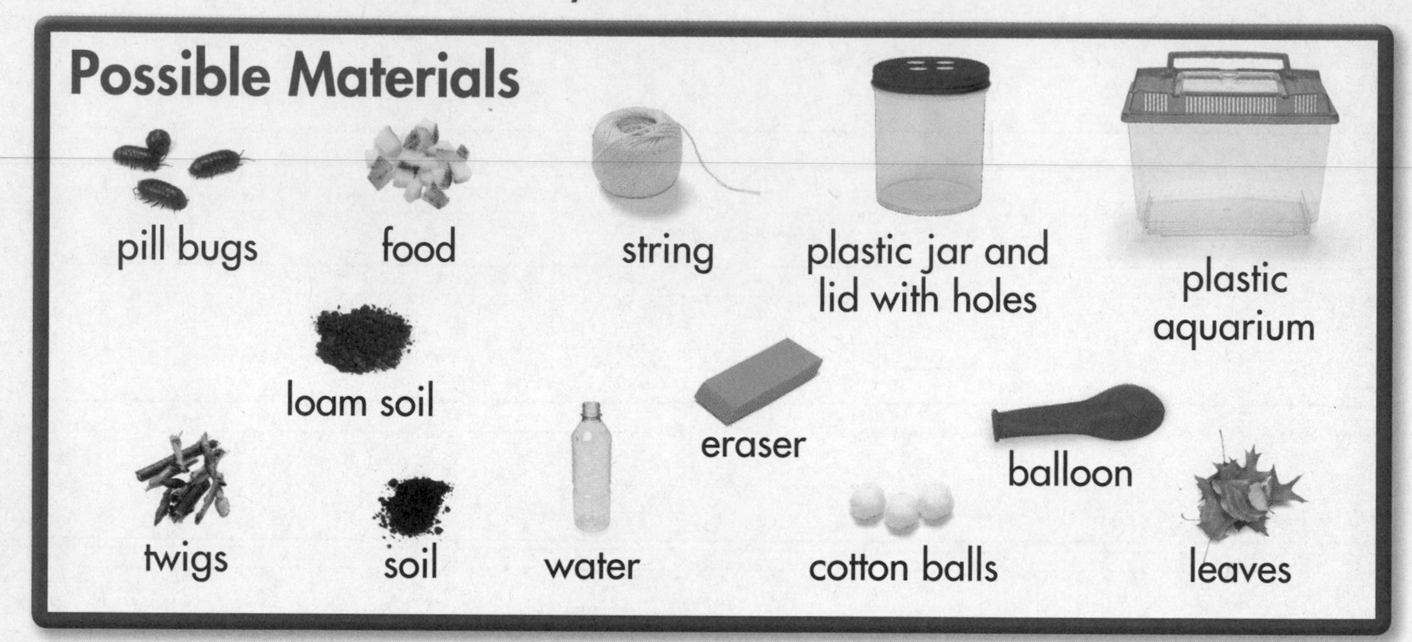

☑ **5.** Tell which need each material meets.

Make and Test

6. Make the habitat you **designed.** Follow your plan.
7. Draw your pill bugs in the habitat.

Record and Share

☑ **8. Observe** your design for one week.
Observe the habitat.
Observe the pill bugs.

Day Observations	
Day	**Observation**
1	
2	
3	
4	
5	

These pill bugs are shown five times their regular size.

☑ **9.** Compare your habitat with other groups. How were the habitats the same?

☑ **10.** How were the habitats different?

☑ **11.** How could you **redesign** your pill bug habitat?

Performance-Based Assessment

Design a New Hat

- Design a new hat.
- Draw a picture of the hat. Label parts of the hat.
- Tell about your picture.

1.NS.5, 1.DP.8

Write a Poem

- Think of a goal.
- Write a poem about a solution for your goal.

1.DP.2

Test Materials

- Draw lines with a pen, a marker, and a crayon.
- Use an eraser to erase your lines.
- Write a sentence about which material erases best.

1.NS.2

Using Scientific Methods

1. Ask a question.
2. Make a hypothesis.
3. Plan a fair test.
4. Do your test.
5. Collect and record data.
6. Tell your conclusion.

Physical Science

Chapter 3
Matter

How can you describe matter?

What is inside a bubble?

Matter

Try It! How can you use a tool to measure?

Lesson 1 What is matter?
1.1.1

Lesson 2 What are solids, liquids, and gases?
1.1.2

Lesson 3 What is a mixture?
1.1.3

Investigate It! How are objects different?

Tell how you make bubbles.

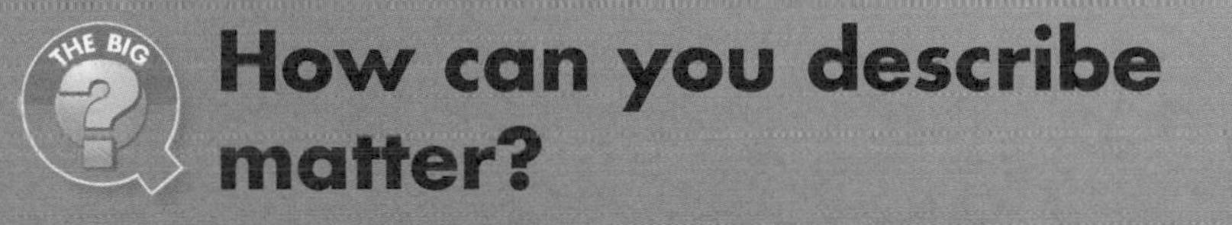

How can you describe matter?

Go to www.myscienceonline.com and click on:

UntamedScience™
Go on a science adventure with the Ecogeeks!

Got it? 60-Second Video
Watch and learn.

Explore It! Animation
Interact with the lab and see what happens!

Vocabulary Smart Cards
Hear and see your vocabulary words online!

Inquiry **Try It!**

How can you use a tool to measure?

Materials

Straw Ruler B

Straw Ruler A

☑ **1.** Use Straw Ruler A.
Measure the width of your desk.
How many straw pieces wide is it?
Record. Measure 3 more things.

Inquiry Skill
You can estimate before you **measure.**

☑ **2.** Use Straw Ruler B. Measure each thing again. Record.

What I Measured	Measured Using Straw Ruler A	Measured Using Straw Ruler B

Explain Your Results

3. Infer Why were your **measurements** different?

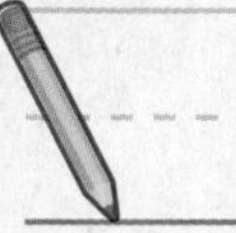

4. Why measure with the same size unit?

1.NS.6 Make and use simple equipment and tools to gather data and extend the senses. **1.NS.7** Recognize a fair test.

Let's Read **Science!**

Main Idea and Details

The **main idea** is what the sentences are about.

Details tell about the main idea.

A Clay Cat

The object is a clay cat.

The ears are blue triangles.

The whiskers are long and yellow.

Practice It!

Write two details that tell about the main idea.

Main Idea

The object is a clay cat.

Lesson 1

What is matter?

Envision It!

1.1.1 Use all senses as appropriate to identify the component parts of objects and the materials from which they are made. (Also 1.NS.3, 1.NS.4)

Draw another object in the classroom.

my planet Diary Fact or Fiction?

Read Together

Pumice is a rock. Do you think it will sink or float?

Pumice forms when lava from a volcano cools and hardens quickly. Pumice has lots of bubble holes. These holes are filled with air. The air bubbles cannot escape. Pumice floats because it is full of air bubbles.

pumice

Sometimes the bubble holes fill with clay. Will pumice filled with clay float? Why?

Tell about the object.

I will know how to describe matter.
I will know how to group matter.

Words to Know

matter
weight
mass

Matter

Matter is anything that takes up space.
Matter has mass.
Mass is the amount of matter in an object.
The table is matter and has mass.

The table has more mass than the glue bottles.

Main Idea and Details **Write** two details about matter.

Objects and Matter

All objects are made of matter.
You can describe objects many ways.
Objects can be different colors.
Objects can be different
sizes and shapes.
Objects can be hard or soft.
The red marble is round and hard.

Label the objects.
square purple small

Draw an X on
two soft objects.

Describe and Group Objects

Objects can feel different.
The wall feels smooth.
Objects can be heavy or light.
Weight is how heavy an object is.
The books are heavy.

You can group objects by how
they are alike.
The balls and marbles are alike.
The balls and marbles are round.

Tell how you can sort the objects in the room by color.

Tell how you would order the orange ball, softball, and tennis ball from heavy to light. **Tell** which object has the greatest mass.

More Ways to Describe Objects

Objects can float or sink.

Float means to stay on top of a liquid.

Sink means to fall to the bottom of a liquid.

Lemonade is a liquid.

The ice cubes float in the lemonade.

Objects can be different temperatures.

The lemonade is cold.

Objects can be made of different materials.

The sink is metal.

The timer is plastic.

Draw an X on something that sinks.

Circle something that is hot.

Lightning Lab

Measure Length

Length is another way to describe objects. Use paper clips to measure your desk. How wide is it? How long is it? Do the same thing using your hand, your shoe, or cubes.

Write two words that describe the lemonade.

Lesson 2

What are solids, liquids, and gases?

1.1.2 Characterize materials as solid or liquid, investigate their properties, record observations and explain the choices to others based on evidence (e.g., physical properties). (Also 1.NS.5)

Envision It!

Draw an X on an object that is filled with a gas.

Inquiry Explore It!

Materials

- rock in sealed plastic bag
- water in sealed plastic bag
- air in sealed plastic bag

What are the states of matter like?

☐ **1.** Gently squeeze each bag. **Observe.**

☐ **2.** Did the shape of the rock change?
Did the shape of the water change?
Did the shape of the air change?

Explain Your Results

3. Classify How are solids, liquids, and gases different?

 1.1.1 Use all senses as appropriate to identify the component parts of objects and the materials from which they are made.

I will know that matter can be a solid, a liquid, or a gas.

Words to Know

solid liquid gas
freeze melt boil

Solids

Matter can be a solid, liquid, or gas.
A **solid** has its own shape.
A solid has its own size.
A solid does not change shape when it is moved.

The box is a solid.
The toys are solids.

Tell what happens to the shape of a toy when you pick it up.

Main Idea and Details

Write two details about solids.

Liquids and Gases

A **liquid** takes the shape of its container.
You can pour a liquid.
Water is a liquid.

A **gas** can change shape and size.
A gas takes the shape of its container.
A gas fills all of its container.
You cannot see most gases.
Air is a gas.

Circle something that contains a liquid. **Tell** one thing about each kind of matter.

At-Home Lab

Kinds of Matter
Gather objects.
Put the solids together.
Put the liquids together.
Tell which objects contain a gas.

How Matter Changes

Matter can change form.

Water freezes into ice when it gets very cold.

Freeze means to change from a liquid to a solid.

Ice melts when it gets warm.

Melt means to change from a solid to a liquid.

Water can evaporate when it boils.

Boil means to heat a liquid until it becomes a gas.

Circle a liquid that is changing into a gas.

Draw a solid that would melt in the sun.

Lesson 3

What is a mixture?

Envision It!

1.1.3 Predict the results of, and experiment with methods (e.g., sieving, evaporation) for separating solids and liquids based on their physical properties. (Also 1.NS.3)

Tell how you could get the coins.

Inquiry **Explore It!**

How can you separate solids and liquids?

Materials

cup with water

spoon

lemonade powder

1. Put $\frac{1}{2}$ spoonful of lemonade powder into a cup with water. Stir. **Observe.**
2. Wait 3 days. Observe. **Record.**

Explain Your Results

3. **Infer** How did the solid separate from the water?

1.1.2 Characterize materials as solid or liquid, investigate their properties, record observations and explain the choices to others based on evidence (e.g. physical properties). **1.NS.2** Conduct investigations that may happen over time as a class, in small groups, or independently.

I will know how to separate a mixture of solids and liquids.

Words to Know

mixture

evaporate

Mixtures

A **mixture** has more than one kind of matter.

A mixture can have solids and liquids.

Soup is a mixture.

The carrots and noodles in soup are solids.

The broth in soup is a liquid.

Circle two solids in the soup.

Screen

You can separate things in a mixture.
You can pour soup into a screen.
The solids stay in the screen.
The liquid drips through the screen.

Look at the picture. **Tell** why the solids stay in the screen.

Main Idea and Details **Write** two details about how to separate solids and liquids with a screen.

Evaporate

You leave soup out for a long time.
The broth evaporates.

Evaporate means to change from a liquid to a gas.
The gas does not stay in the bowl.
The broth separates from the carrots and noodles.

Underline what it means to evaporate.

Draw an arrow to show where the broth went.

At-Home Lab

Find a Mixture
Look in the refrigerator. Tell what mixtures you find.

Inquiry **Investigate It!**

How are objects different?

Follow a Procedure

☑ **1. Observe** Look at all the objects.

☑ **2. Classify**

Put the solid objects together.

Put the liquid objects together.

Inquiry Skill
To **observe** means to look carefully.

1.1.2 Characterize materials as solid or liquid, investigate their properties, record observations and explain the choices to others based on evidence (e.g., physical properties). (Also **1.NS.1**)

3. Classify each object as hard or wet.
Use the chart. Make an X for each object.

Observations		
	Hard	**Wet**
Gram cubes		
Metal marbles		
Ice cube		
Water		
Milk		

Analyze and Conclude

4. **Draw a Conclusion** How are these solids the same? How are these liquids the same?

5. UNLOCK THE BIG ? What two states of matter did you **observe**? Which did you not observe?

Science in Your Backyard

1.1.2

Describe Matter

You can learn about solids, liquids, and gases where you live. Go outside or to a park with an adult. Look around. What solids do you see? What liquids do you see? What clues do you see to know that there are gases?

Describe a solid, a liquid, or a clue about a gas that you see.

What is it?	What is it like?

Vocabulary Smart Cards

matter
mass
weight
solid
liquid
gas
freeze
melt
boil
mixture
evaporate

Play a Game!

Cut out the cards.

Work with a partner.

Cover up the words on each card.

Look at the picture and guess the word.

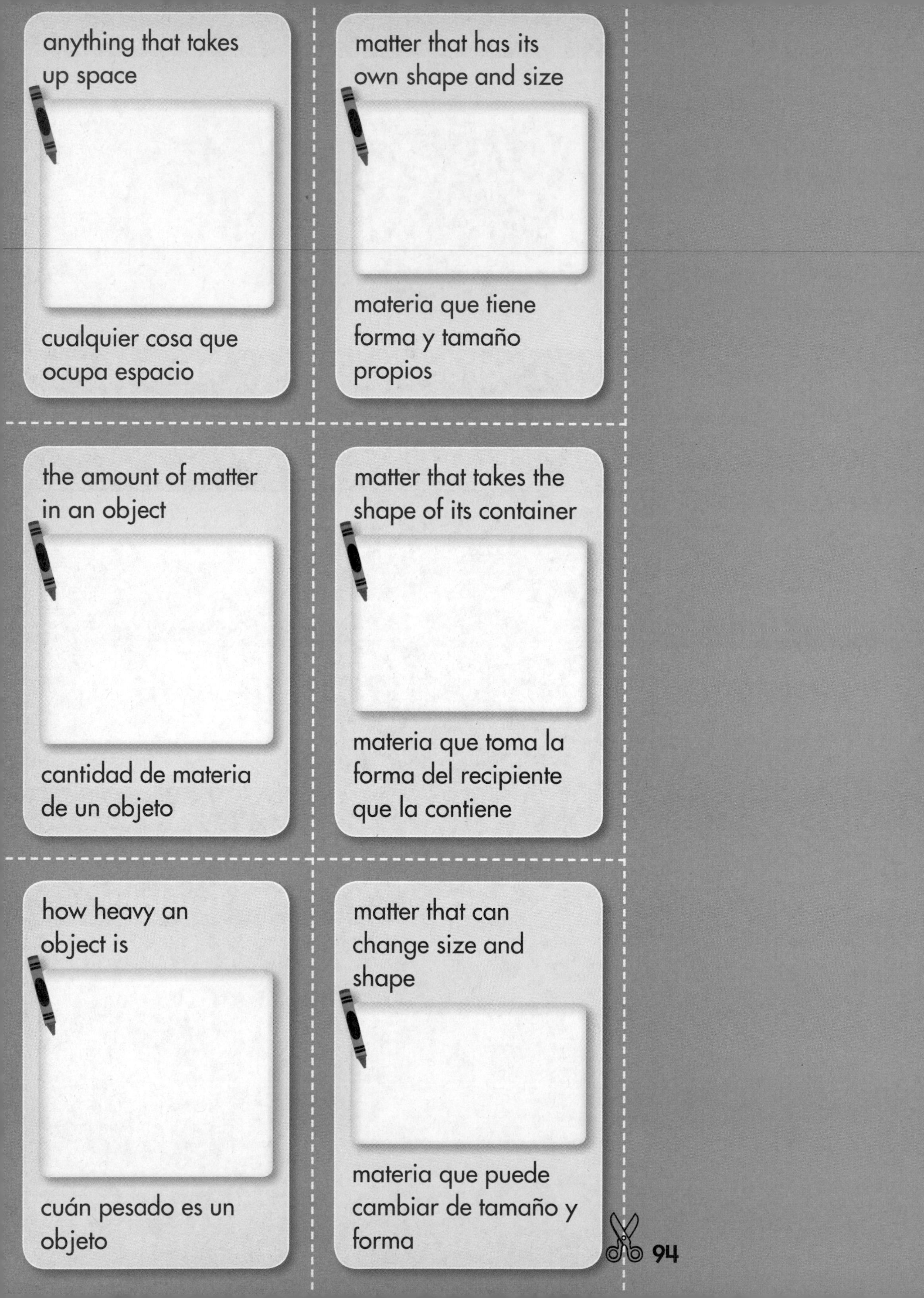
anything that takes up space
cualquier cosa que ocupa espacio
matter that has its own shape and size
materia que tiene forma y tamaño propios
the amount of matter in an object
cantidad de materia de un objeto
matter that takes the shape of its container
materia que toma la forma del recipiente que la contiene
how heavy an object is
cuán pesado es un objeto
matter that can change size and shape
materia que puede cambiar de tamaño y forma

mixture
mezcla
freeze
congelar
evaporate
evaporarse
melt
derretir
boil
hervir

to change from a liquid to a solid
cambiar de líquido a sólido
more than one kind of matter
más de un tipo de materia
to change from a solid to a liquid
cambiar de sólido a líquido
to change from a liquid to a gas
cambiar de líquido a gas
to heat a liquid until it becomes a gas
calentar un líquido hasta que se convierte en gas

Chapter 3
Study Guide

How can you describe matter?

Indiana

Lesson 1

What is matter?

- Matter takes up space and has mass.
- Weight is one way to describe objects.

Lesson 2

What are solids, liquids, and gases?

- Matter can be a solid, liquid, or gas.
- Water can freeze, melt, or boil.

Lesson 3

What is a mixture?

- A mixture can have solids and liquids.
- Liquids evaporate to separate from solids.

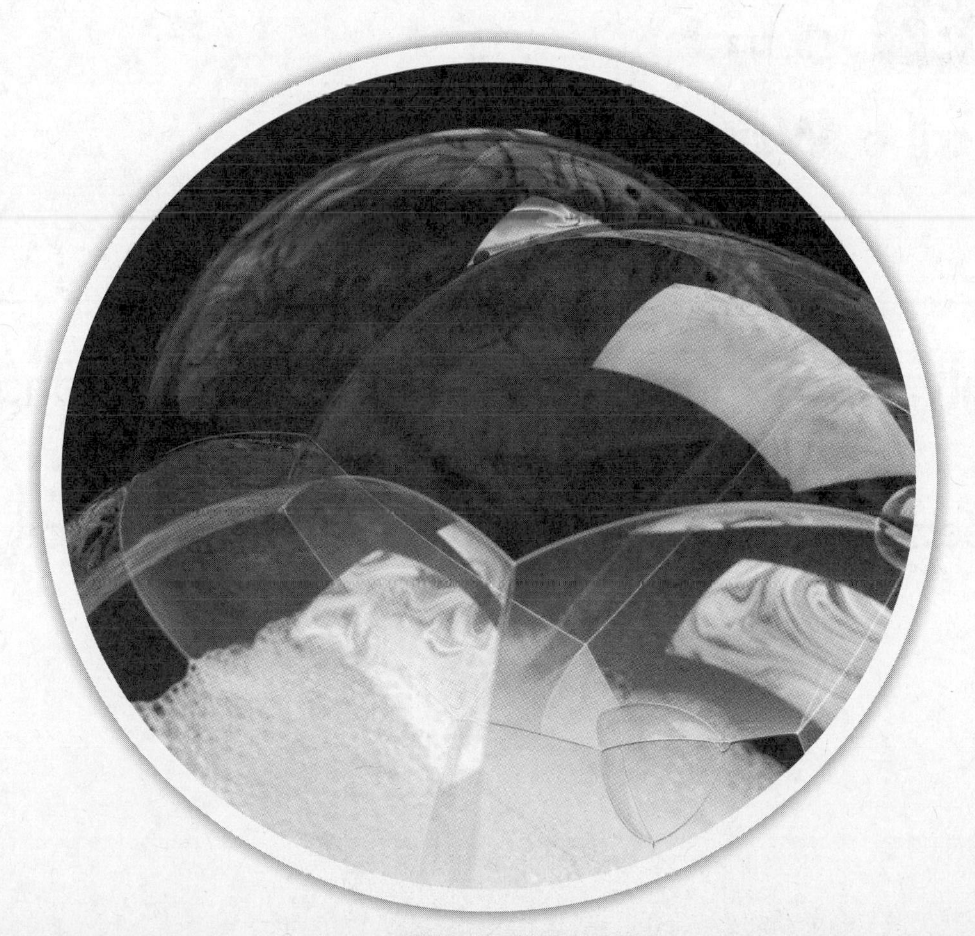

Chapter Review

REVIEW THE BIG ? How can you describe matter?

Lesson 1

1.1.1

1. What takes up space? **Circle** the letter.

A. force
B. speed
C. matter
D. direction

2. Classify How can you group the blocks in the picture?

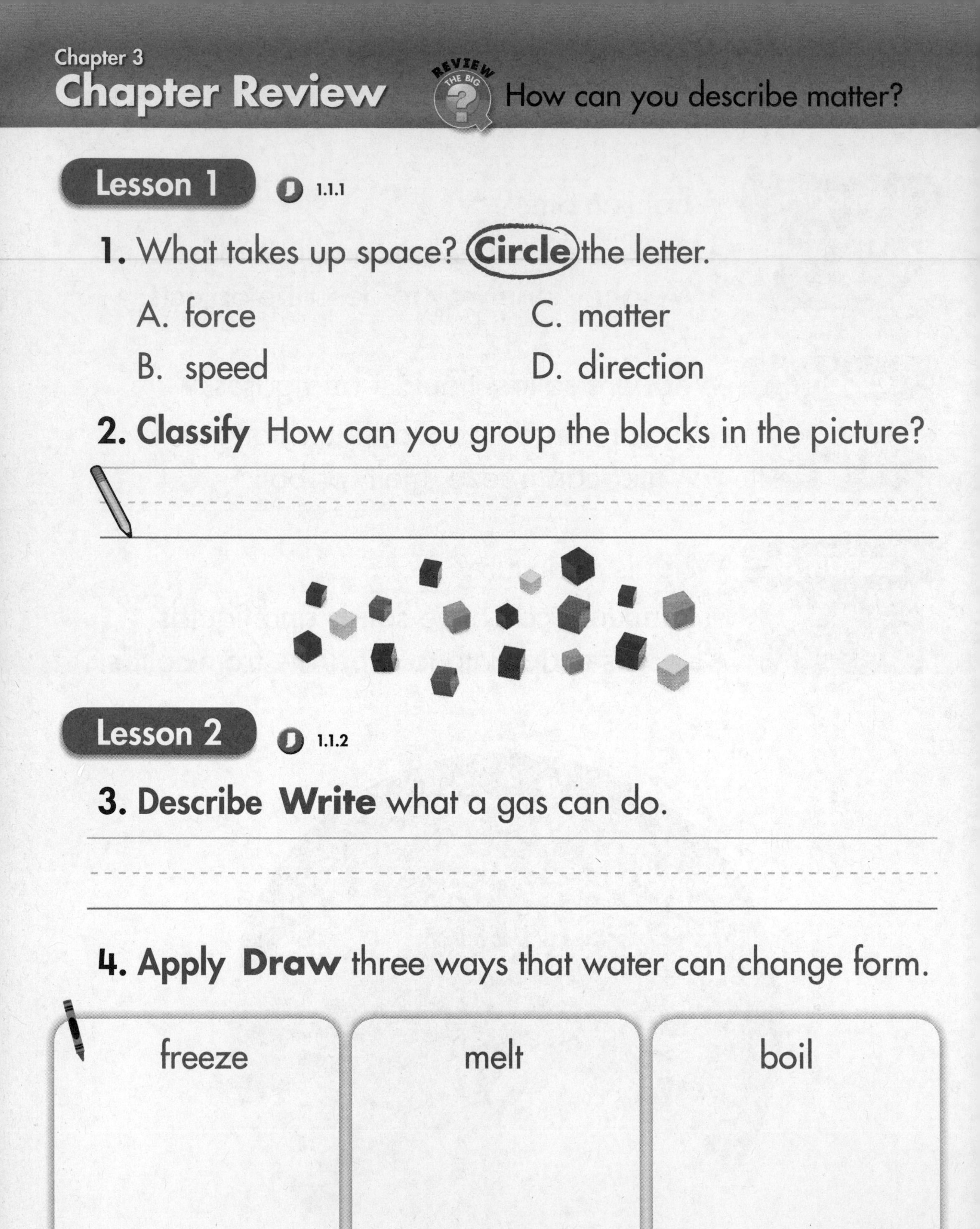

Lesson 2

1.1.2

3. Describe Write what a gas can do.

4. Apply Draw three ways that water can change form.

freeze	melt	boil

Lesson 3

5. Vocabulary Circle a way to separate solids and liquids.

6. Main Idea and Details

Underline two details below.

You can separate solids and liquids in a mixture. You can separate them with a screen. You can let the liquid evaporate.

Got it?

Stop! I need help with

Go! Now I know

Inquiry **Apply It!** Using Scientific Methods

Which objects will float?

Materials

objects

water

Inquiry Skill
When you **classify**, you sort things.

Some objects float. Other objects sink.

Ask a question.

Which objects will float?

Make a prediction.

1. Choose an object. Tell what you think.

The ______________ will **(float / sink)**.

Plan a fair test.

Use all of the objects.

Make sure to clean up spills!

Make predictions before you test.

Design your test.

2. List your steps.

1.1.2 Characterize materials as solid or liquid, investigate their properties, record observations and explain the choices to others based on evidence (e.g. physical properties). **1.NS.6** Make and use simple equipment and tools to gather data and extend the senses. (Also **1.1.1**)

Do your test.

☑ **3.** Follow your steps.

Collect and record data.

☑ **4.** Fill in the chart.

Tell your conclusion.

5. Classify Which objects float?

6. Which objects sink?

Performance-Based Assessment

Group Objects

- Group objects such as buttons or blocks by the materials they are made of.
- Label the groups. Write a sentence about each group.

1.1.1

Cool a Balloon

- Blow up a balloon.
- Find out if the size of the balloon changes when it is in cold water.

1.1.2

Order Objects by Mass

- Choose three objects.
- Predict which object will have the least mass and which will have the most mass.
- Use a pan balance to test your predictions.

1.1.2

Using Scientific Methods

1. Ask a question.
2. Make a hypothesis.
3. Plan a fair test.
4. Do your test.
5. Collect and record data.
6. Tell your conclusion.

Earth and Space Science

Chapter 4

Soil

What is Earth made of?

Where does the soil come from?

Indiana

Chapter 4

Soil

Try It! What makes up soil?

Lesson 1 What is on Earth?
1.2.3

Lesson 2 How is soil made?
1.2.4

Lesson 3 What are some kinds of soil?
1.2.1, 1.2.2

Investigate It! How are soils different?

THE BIG ? **What is Earth made of?**

Go to www.myscienceonline.com and click on:

UntamedScience™
Watch the Ecogeeks in this wild video.

Got it? 60-Second Video
Take one minute to learn science!

Science Songs
Sing along with science songs!

my planet Diary
Connect to the world!

Envision It!
See what you already know about science.

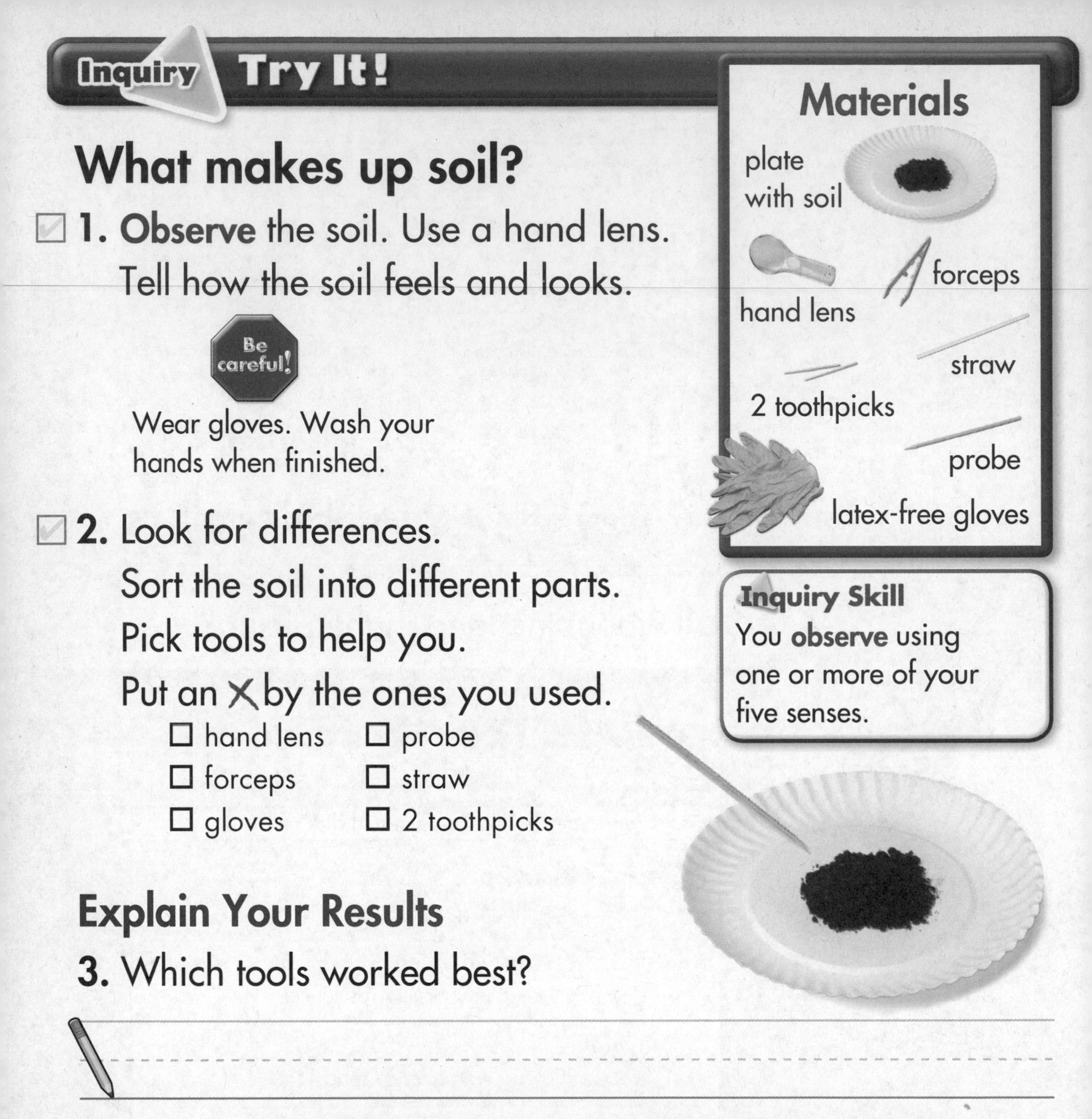

What makes up soil?

1. **Observe** the soil. Use a hand lens. Tell how the soil feels and looks.

   Wear gloves. Wash your hands when finished.

2. Look for differences. Sort the soil into different parts. Pick tools to help you. Put an X by the ones you used.

   - ☐ hand lens
   - ☐ forceps
   - ☐ gloves
   - ☐ probe
   - ☐ straw
   - ☐ 2 toothpicks

Inquiry Skill
You **observe** using one or more of your five senses.

Explain Your Results

3. Which tools worked best?

4. **Draw a Conclusion** What makes up soil?

1.2.2 Choose, test, and use tools to separate soil samples into component parts. **1.2.3** Observe a variety of soil samples and describe in words and pictures the soil properties in terms of color, particle size and shape, texture, and recognizable living and nonliving items in the soil. **1.NS.6** Make and use simple equipment and tools to gather data and extend the senses. (Also **1.1.1, 1.NS.1**)

Appalachian Mountains

Compare and Contrast

You **compare** when you tell how things are alike.
You **contrast** when you tell how things are different.

Mountains

Mountains are very high.
The Rocky Mountains are rough.
The Appalachian Mountains are not.
The Rocky Mountains are higher than the Appalachian Mountains.

Rocky Mountains

Practice It!

Write how the mountains are alike and different.

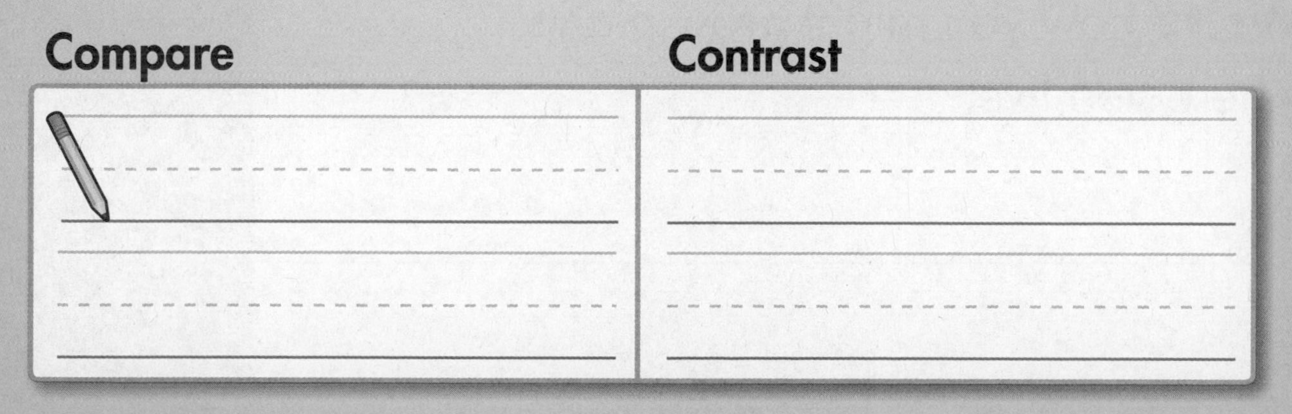

Lesson 1

What is on Earth?

Envision It!

1.2.3 Observe a variety of soil samples and describe in words and pictures the soil properties in terms of color, particle size and shape, texture, and recognizable living and nonliving items in the soil. (Also 1.NS.3)

Draw another kind of land or water.

my planet Diary

Connections

Read Together

Long ago people known as the Incas lived in the mountains in South America. It was hard to grow crops in the mountains. The Incas built flat pieces of land called terraces so they could grow crops. Today some people do not have land to grow crops and other plants. They use pots and planters.

Write how you might grow plants where you live.

UNLOCK THE BIG ? I will know that land, water, and living things are found on Earth.

Word to Know

soil

Land, Water, and Air

Earth is made of many things.
Earth has land.
Earth has water.
The surface of Earth has more water than land.
Earth has air all around it.

Color the land green.
Color the water blue.

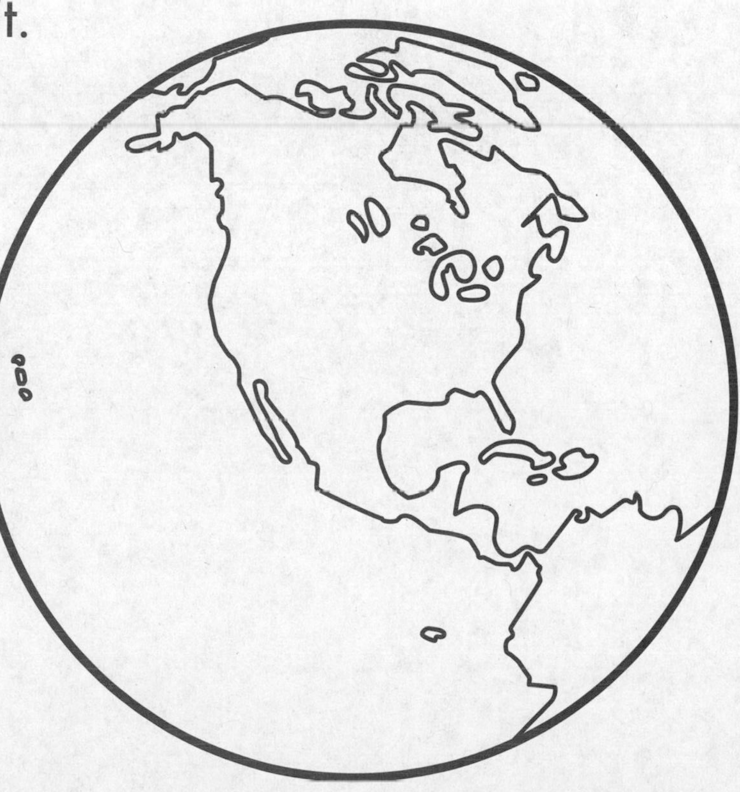

Kinds of Land

Earth has many different kinds of land. Plains are large, flat areas of land. Hills are where the land gets higher. Mountains are the highest kind of land. An island is land with water all around it.

Label the plains, mountains, and island.

The Blue Ridge Mountains rise above the land around them.

Rocks and Soil

Earth's land has rocks and soil.
Rocks are hard.
Rocks can be many colors.
Soil is the top layer of Earth.
Soil can be soft.

rocks and soil

Underline two things that are found on Earth.

Compare and Contrast **Write** one way rocks and soil are different.

At-Home Lab

Types of Landforms
Draw one kind of land near where you live. Draw another kind of land. Write how they are the same. Write how they are different.

Water on Earth

Earth has many places with water.

A river is water that flows across land.

Lakes have land all around them.

Oceans are large areas of salt water.

Oceans cover most of Earth.

Match the word to the picture.

Draw a line.

river lake ocean

Living Things

Living things are on land.

Living things are in soil.

Living things are in water.

Circle living things on land.

Draw an X on living things in water.

Lesson 2

How is soil made?

Envision It!

1.2.4 Observe over time the effect of organisms such as earthworms in the formation of soil from dead plants. Discuss the importance of earthworms in soil. (Also 1.NS.4)

Tell how you think the worms help soil.

Inquiry Explore It!

How can earthworms help make soil?

1. Put leaves in the bag. Add soil. Add worms. Close the bag.

Be careful! Wear gloves. Wash your hands when finished.

2. **Observe** the leaves and soil for 4 days. **Record** the changes.

Explain Your Results

3. **Infer** What happened to the leaves?

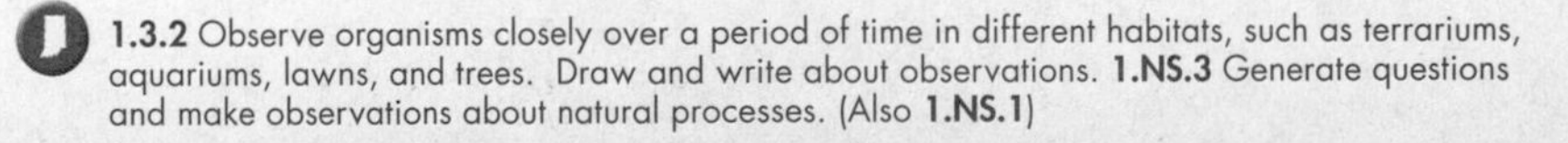

1.3.2 Observe organisms closely over a period of time in different habitats, such as terrariums, aquariums, lawns, and trees. Draw and write about observations. 1.NS.3 Generate questions and make observations about natural processes. (Also 1.NS.1)

UNLOCK THE BIG Q I will know how soil forms. I will know how earthworms help make soil.

Word to Know

earthworm

How Soil Forms

This is a compost pile. The food and plant parts will form soil.

Many things make up soil.
Soil has pieces of rocks.
Soil has parts of dead plants and animals.
Soil forms when these things mix together.
Wind and water can help form soil.
Wind and water mix together parts of soil.

Write what could help this compost pile form soil.

Earthworms

Earthworms are animals.
Earthworms live in soil.
Earthworms help form soil.
Earthworms mix soil when they move.
Earthworms mix soil when they eat.
An earthworm takes soil into its mouth.
Soil moves through the earthworm.
This helps dead plants become soil.
Earthworms move nutrients through soil.
Plants need these nutrients to grow.

Underline how earthworms help plants.

Draw an arrow to show how soil moves through the earthworm.

Go Green

Compost
Look around your classroom. List things that can make compost.

Compare and Contrast **Write** what earthworms and wind both do to soil.

Lesson 3

What are some kinds of soil?

Envision It!

1.2.1 Observe and compare properties of sand, clay, silt and organic matter. Look for evidence of sand, clay, silt and organic matter as components of soil samples. 1.2.2 Choose, test, and use tools to separate soil samples into component parts. (Also 1.2.3, 1.NS.1, 1.NS.5)

Circle where you think the plant would grow best.

Inquiry Explore It!

What are different soils like?

☑ 1. Put a spoonful of each soil on a plate.

☑ 2. **Observe.** Draw. Show colors. Tell how each soil feels.

silt	sandy
loam	clay

Do you see anything alive or that was once living?

Wash your hands when done.

Explain Your Results

3. **Communicate** How is loam soil different?

____

1.1.1 Use all senses as appropriate to identify the component parts of objects and the materials from which they are made. **1.NS.2** Conduct investigations that may happen over time as a class, in small groups, or independently. (Also **1.NS.6**)

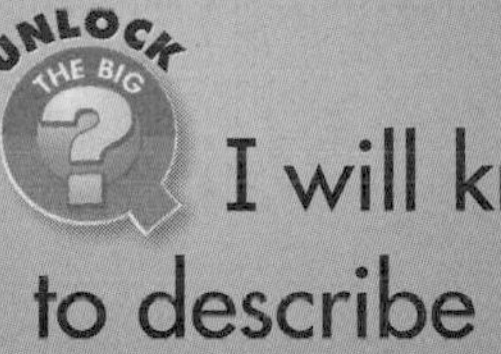

I will know how to describe soil.

Word to Know

humus

Soil Layers

Soil covers the land.
Soil has layers.
The layers have different colors.
The layers have different textures.
Texture is how something feels.
Plants and animals only live in the top layers of soil.

Look at the picture from top to bottom.
Tell what you see.

Deeper layers of soil have more rocks in them.

Nonliving and Living Parts

Some parts of soil are nonliving.

Soil has tiny bits of rock.

It has humus also.

Humus is small pieces of dead plants and animals.

It has air and water too.

Some parts of soil are living.

Animals and other small living things live in soil.

Draw an X on two living or once living parts of soil in the picture.

Circle a nonliving part of the soil.

humus

Clay Soil

clay

Clay can feel smooth.
Clay can feel soft.
Clay can feel sticky.
Some clay is red.
Clay soil does not have a lot of air.
Most plants do not grow well in clay soil.

The nutrient iron makes the clay red. A nutrient is something living things need to live and grow.

Underline the words that tell about the texture of clay.

A seed is planted in clay soil. Will it grow? Why or why not?

At-Home Lab

Describe Soil
Work with an adult. Look at some soil. What color is it? How does it feel? What parts do you see?

Sandy Soil

Sandy soil is very loose.
It feels dry and rough.
Often sandy soil is tan.
Most plants do not grow well
in sandy soil.
Sandy soil does not hold water well.

sandy soil

Compare and Contrast

Write two ways that sandy and
clay soils are different.

Deserts have sandy soil.

Gardens have loam soil.

loam

silt

Loam

Loam has sand and clay.

Loam has humus and silt too.

Silt has small grains.

Loam feels wet.

Loam is often dark brown.

Loam has the right amount of water and air.

Plants grow well in loam soil.

Circle what is in loam.

Draw how you could use loam.

Inquiry **Investigate It!**

How are soils different?

Follow a Procedure

☐ 1. **Measure** 50 mL of water.

☐ 2. **Investigate** Hold a filter cup with sandy soil over a plastic cup. Pour the water into the soil. Measure the time until water first drips out.

Materials

sandy soil in filter cup*
clay soil in filter cup*
loam soil in filter cup*
(*prepared by teacher)

water

timer

3 plastic cups

graduated cylinder

Inquiry Skill
Scientists make careful observations when they carry out an **investigation.**

Be careful! Wash your hands when finished!

1.2.1 Observe and compare properties of sand, clay, silt and organic matter. Look for evidence of sand, clay, silt and organic matter as components of soil samples. **1.NS.2** Conduct investigations that may happen over time as a class, in small groups, or independently.

☑ **3.** Repeat Steps 1 and 2 with clay soil and loam.

☑ **4. Record.**

Water Drip Times

Soil	How much water? (mL)	Time when water first drips (seconds)
Sandy soil		
Clay soil		
Loam soil		

Analyze and Conclude

5. Interpret Data Which soil let water through fastest?

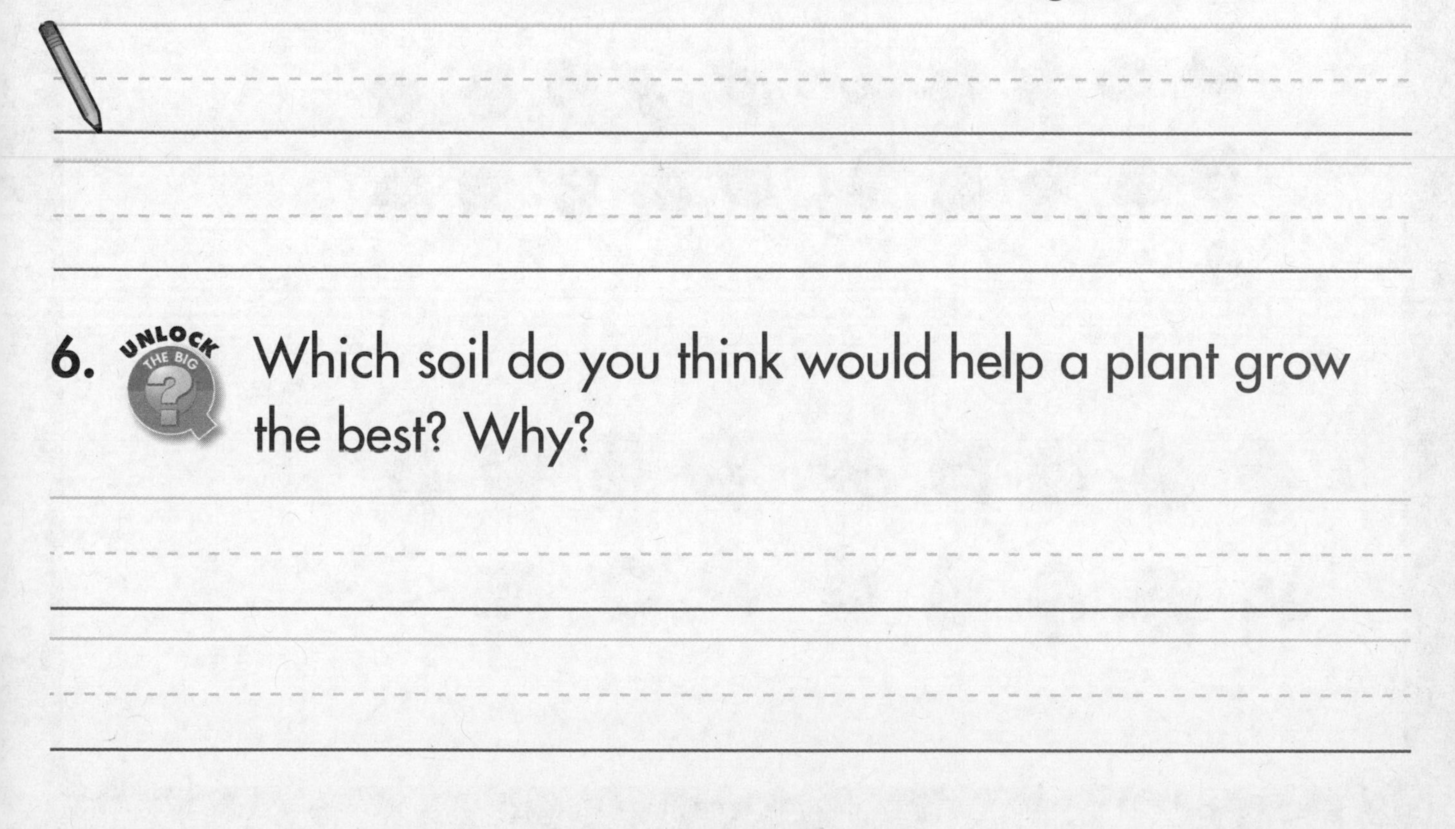

6. Which soil do you think would help a plant grow the best? Why?

Do the math!

Count Rocks

Circle groups of ten rocks.
Count the tens.
Count the ones.
Add the number of rocks in the groups together.

1.

2.

3.

Vocabulary Smart Cards

soil
earthworm
humus

Play a Game!

Cut out the cards.

Work with a group.

Tape a card to the back of each group member.

Have each member guess what his or her word is by giving clues.

soil

suelo

earthworm

lombriz

humus

humus

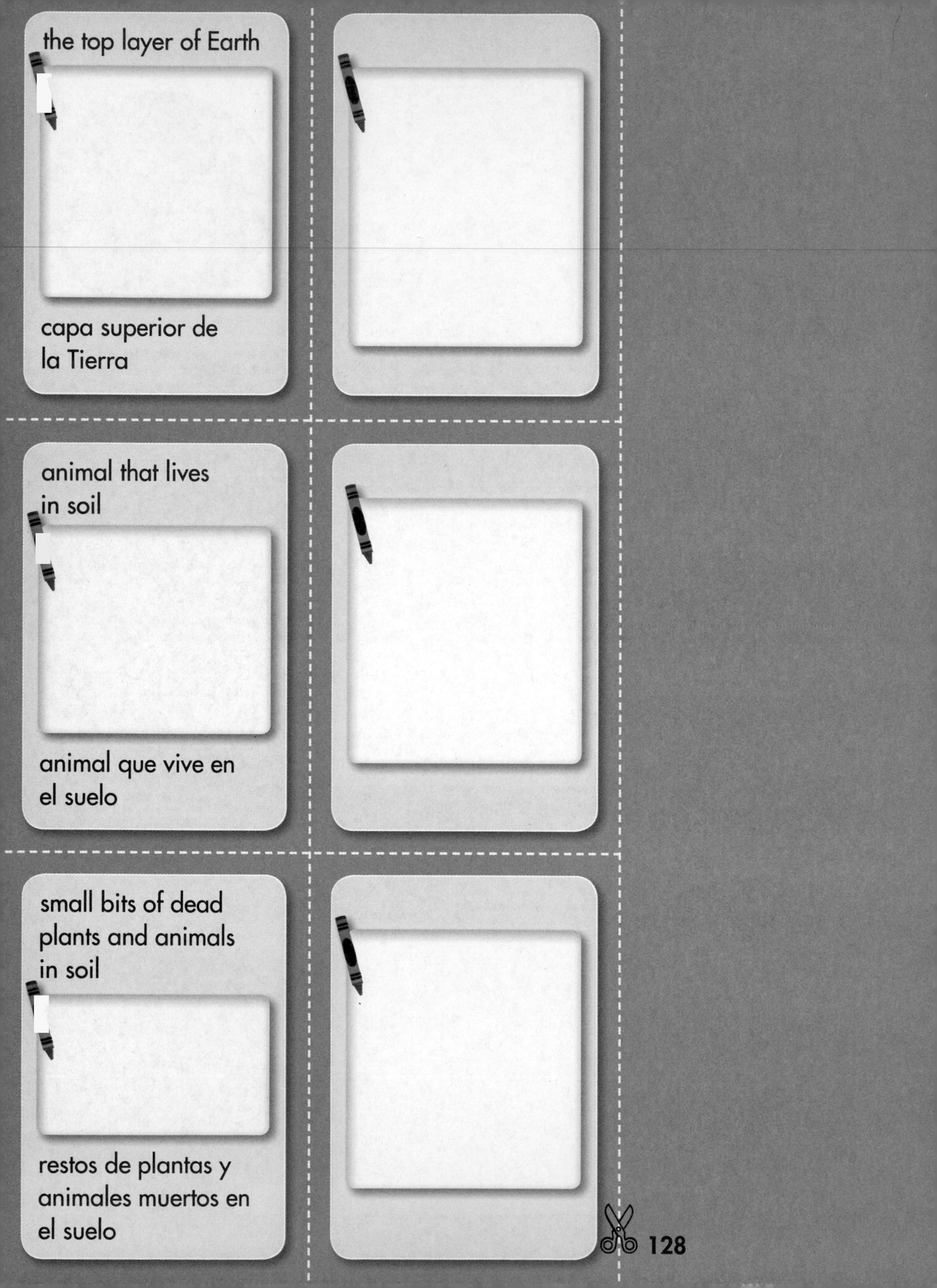
the top layer of Earth
capa superior de la Tierra
animal that lives in soil
animal que vive en el suelo
small bits of dead plants and animals in soil
restos de plantas y animales muertos en el suelo

Chapter 4

Study Guide

REVIEW THE BIG ? What is Earth made of?

Indiana

Lesson 1

What is on Earth?

- Earth has different kinds of land and water.
- Rocks and soil are on Earth's surface.

Lesson 2

How is soil made?

- Many parts mix together to form soil.
- Earthworms mix and move nutrients in soil.

Lesson 3

What are some kinds of soil?

- Soil is often found in layers.
- Soil has tiny bits of rock and humus.

Chapter Review

THE BIG ? REVIEW What is Earth made of?

Lesson 1

1.2.3

1. **Exemplify** **Draw** two things that are found on Earth.

2. __________ is the top layer of Earth. **Circle** the letter.

A. Soil
B. A lake
C. A mountain
D. The sun

Lesson 2

1.2.4

3. **Infer** Why are earthworms important to plants?

4. **Summarize** **Draw** an X on two parts of soil.

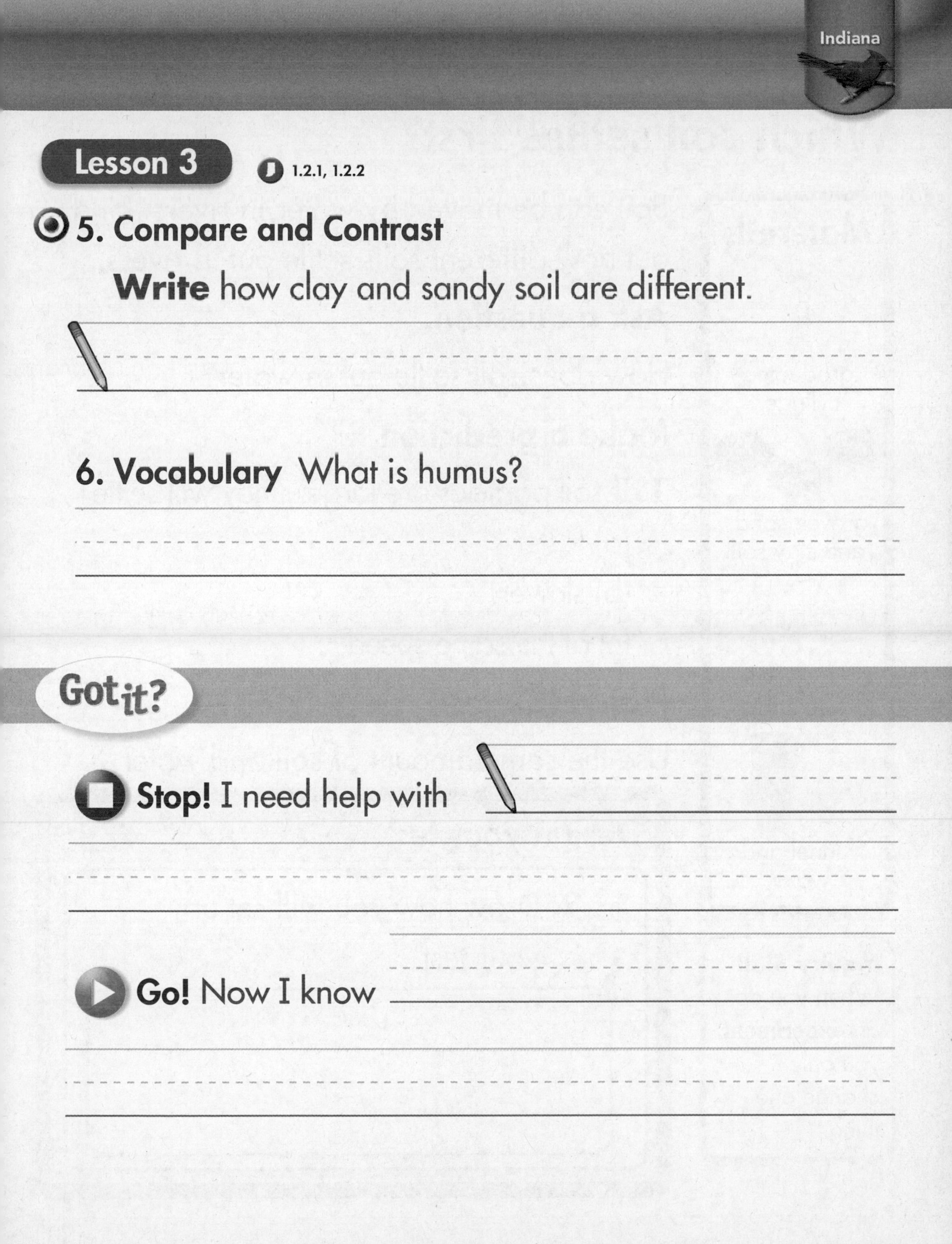

Lesson 3 1.2.1, 1.2.2

5. **Compare and Contrast**

Write how clay and sandy soil are different.

6. **Vocabulary** What is humus?

Got it?

Stop! I need help with

Go! Now I know

Which soil settles first?

Soil can be moved by water in rivers. Find out how different soils settle out in rivers.

Ask a question.

How does soil settle out in water?

Make a prediction.

1. If soil particles are larger, they will settle
   (a) faster.
   (b) slower.
   (c) at the same speed.

Plan a fair test.

Use the same amount of soil and water.

Design your test.

2. Draw how you will set up your test.

1.NS.1 Use a scientific notebook to record predictions, questions, and observations about data with pictures, numbers or in words.
1.NS.7 Recognize a fair test. (Also 1.NS.6)

3. List your steps.

Do your test.

4. Follow your steps.

Collect and record data.

5. Fill in the chart.

Tell your conclusion.

6. Compare your prediction with your results.

Performance-Based Assessment

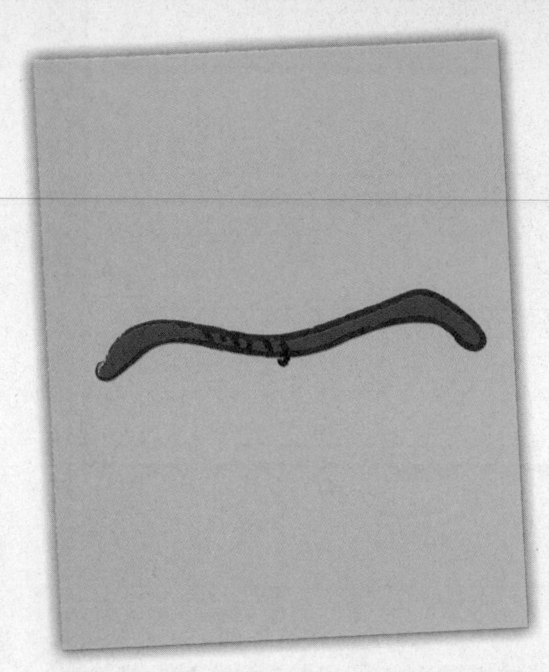

Write a Song

- Write a song about soil.
- Tell how different soils look.
- Tell how different soils feel.

1.2.3

Make a Poster

- Draw an earthworm.
- Write two sentences about how earthworms help soil.
- Use your sentences and picture to make a poster.

1.2.4

Humus and Sand

- Gather samples of humus and sand.
- Add water to each sample.
- Record how the water changes the humus and sand.

1.2.1

Using Scientific Methods

1. Ask a question.
2. Make a hypothesis.
3. Plan a fair test.
4. Do your test.
5. Collect and record data.
6. Tell your conclusion.

Life Science

Chapter 5
Plants, Animals, and Their Habitats

What do living things need?

Where does a cow get food?

Vocabulary Smart Cards

need
nutrients
shelter
habitat
forest
terrarium
desert
wetland
ocean
aquarium
classify

Play a Game!

Cut out the cards.

Put one set word side up.

Put another set word side down.

Match the word with the definition.

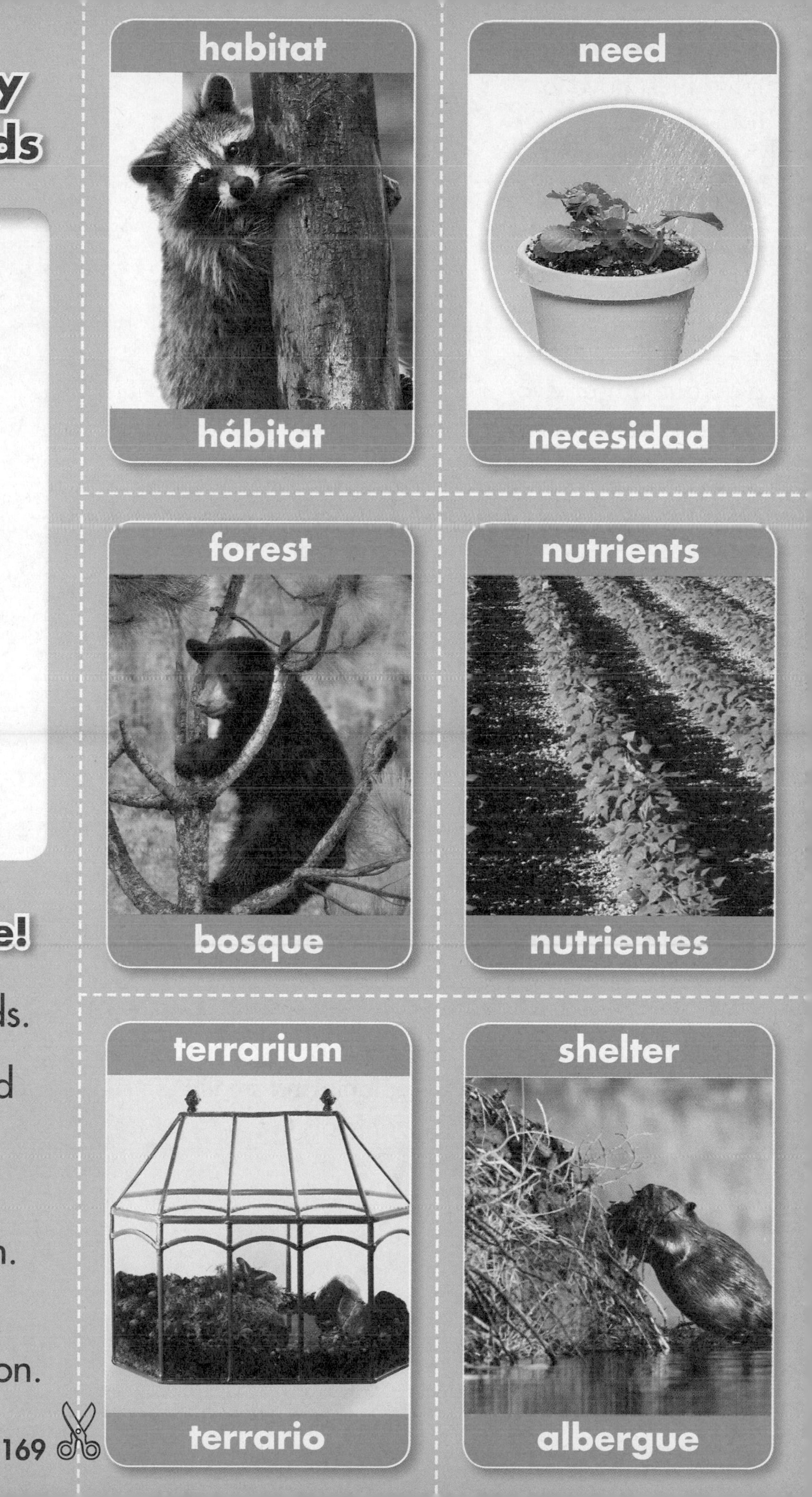

something a living thing must have to live

algo que un ser vivo necesita para vivir

where a plant or animal lives

donde vive una planta o un animal

materials that living things need

sustancias que los seres vivos necesitan

land that has many trees and other plants

terreno que tiene muchos árboles y otras plantas

a safe place

lugar seguro

a glass tank where plants and small animals live

tanque de vidrio donde viven plantas y animales pequeños

aquarium
acuario
desert
desierto
classify
clasificar
wetland
pantanal
ocean
océano

land that is very dry
tierra que es
muy seca
a water habitat in a
glass tank or bowl
hábitat de agua en
una tanque de vidrio
o en un tazón
habitat that is
covered in water
hábitat cubierto
de agua
to group things
agrupar cosas
a large salty body of
water
cuerpo grande de
agua salada

Metric and Customary Measurements

Science uses the metric system to measure things. Metric measurement is used around the world. Here is how different metric measurements compare to customary measurements.

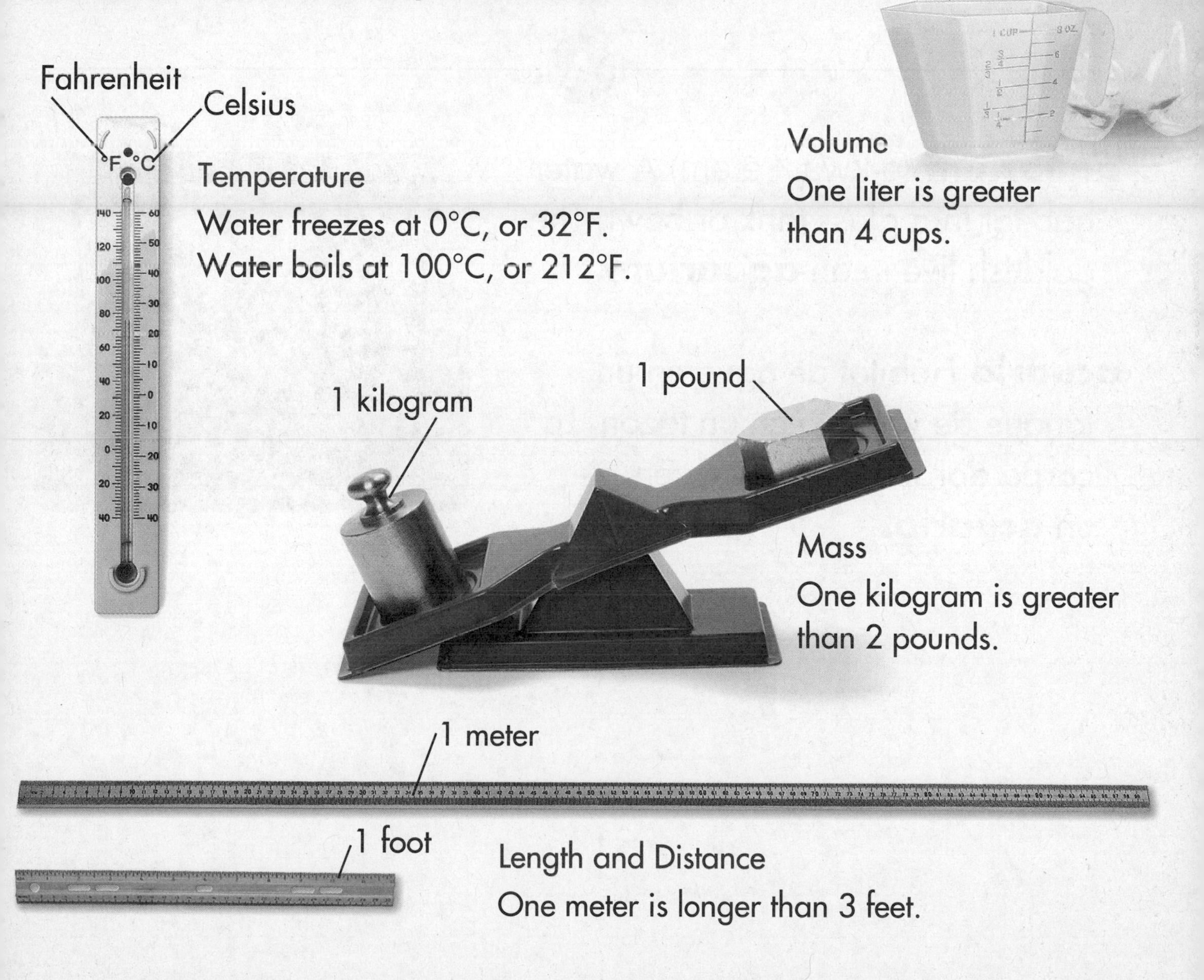

Temperature
Water freezes at 0°C, or 32°F.
Water boils at 100°C, or 212°F.

Volume
One liter is greater than 4 cups.

Mass
One kilogram is greater than 2 pounds.

Length and Distance
One meter is longer than 3 feet.

Glossary

The glossary uses letters and signs to show how words are pronounced. The mark ′ is placed after a syllable with a primary or heavy accent. The mark ′ is placed after a syllable with a secondary or lighter accent.

To hear these vocabulary words and definitions, you can refer to the AudioText CD, or log on to the digital path's Vocabulary Smart Cards.

Pronunciation Key

a	in hat	ō	in open	sh	in she
ā	in age	ȯ	in all	th	in thin
â	in care	ô	in order	ᴛʜ	in then
ä	in far	oi	in oil	zh	in measure
e	in let	ou	in out	ə	= a in about
ē	in equal	u	in cup	ə	= e in taken
ėr	in term	u̇	in put	ə	= i in pencil
i	in it	ü	in rule	ə	= o in lemon
ī	in ice	ch	in child	ə	= u in circus
o	in hot	ng	in long		

A

aquarium (ə kwar′ ē əm) A water habitat in a glass tank or bowl. The goldfish live in an **aquarium.**

acuario Hábitat de agua en un tanque de vidrio o en un tazón. La carpa dorada puede vivir en un **acuario.**

B

boil (boil) To heat a liquid until it becomes a gas. The soup began to **boil** after placing it on the fire.

hervir Calentar un líquido hasta que se convierte en gas. La sopa empezó a **hervir** después de ponerla al fuego.

C

classify (klas′ ə fī) To group things. You can **classify** trees.

clasificar Agrupar cosas. Puedes **clasificar** los árboles.

D

data (dā′ tə) Information you collect. You can record **data** about animals.

datos Información que reúnes. Puedes anotar **datos** acerca de los animales.

desert (dez′ ərt) Land that is very dry. Many plants and animals live in the **desert.**

desierto Tierra que es muy seca. En el **desierto** viven muchas plantas y animales diferentes.

E

earthworm (ėrth′ wėrm′) Animal that lives in soil. The **earthworm** moves through the soil.

lombriz Animal que vive en el suelo. La **lombriz** se mueve por el suelo.

evaporate (i vap′ ə rāt) To change from a liquid to a gas. The broth in the soup began to **evaporate.**

evaporarse Cambiar de líquido a gas. El caldo de la sopa comenzó a **evaporarse.**

forest (fôr′ ist) Land that has many trees and other plants. Some bears live in the **forest.**

bosque Terreno que tiene muchos árboles y otras plantas. Algunos osos viven en el **bosque.**

freeze (frēz) To change from a liquid to a solid. We let water **freeze** to make ice cubes.

congelar Cambiar de líquido a sólido. Dejamos **congelar** el agua para hacer cubitos de hielo.

gas (gas) Matter that can change size and shape. The beach toys were full of **gas.**

gas Materia que puede cambiar de tamaño y forma. Los juguetes de playa estaban llenos de **gas.**

goal (gōl) Something you want to do. You have a **goal** to build shelter for the duck.

objetivo Algo que quieres hacer. Tu **objetivo** es construir un albergue para el pato.

H

habitat (hab′ ə tat) Where a plant or animal lives. The raccoon lives in a **habitat.**

hábitat Donde vive una planta o un animal. El mapache vive en un **hábitat.**

humus (hyü′ məs) Small bits of dead plants and animals in soil. Grandmother adds **humus** to the soil to help her plants grow.

humus Restos de plantas y animales muertos en el suelo. Mi abuela le añade **humus** al suelo para ayudar a sus plantas a crecer.

inquiry (in kwī′ rē) Looking for answers. You can use **inquiry** to learn about water.

indagación Buscar respuestas. Puedes hacer una **indagación** para aprender sobre el agua.

investigate (in ves′ tə gāt) To look for answers to questions. Scientists **investigate** to learn about plants.

investigar Buscar respuestas a las preguntas. Los científicos **investigan** para saber más sobre las plantas.

label (lā′ bəl) Shows what something is. **Labels** can show parts of the drawing.

rótulo Palabra que identifica una cosa. Los **rótulos** pueden mostrar las partes del dibujo.

liquid (lik′ wid) Matter that takes the shape of its container. My mother poured the **liquid** into the glasses.

líquido Materia que toma la forma del recipiente que la contiene. Mi mamá puso el **líquido** en los vasos.

mass (mas) The amount of matter in an object. The table has **mass.**

masa Cantidad de materia de un objeto. La mesa tiene **masa.**

matter (mat′ ər) Anything that takes up space. Everything around you is made of **matter.**

materia Cualquier cosa que ocupa espacio. Todo lo que hay a nuestro alrededor está hecho de **materia.**

measure (mezh′ ər) To use a tool to find the size or amount of something. You **measure** how long a pencil is.

medir Usar un instrumento para saber el tamaño o la cantidad de algo. Puedes **medir** la longitud de un lápiz.

melt (melt) To change from a solid to a liquid. The ice began to **melt** in the sun.

derretir Cambiar de sólido a líquido. El hielo empezó a **derretirse** bajo el sol.

mixture (miks′ chər) More than one kind of matter. The carrots, broth, and noodles form a **mixture.**

mezcla Más de un tipo de materia. Las zanahorias, el caldo y los fideos forman una **mezcla.**

natural (nach′ ər əl) Not made by people. Fruit and wood are **natural.**

natural No hecho por las personas. Las frutas y la madera son **naturales.**

need (nēd) Something a living thing must have to live. Plants grow when their **needs** are met.

necesidad Algo que un ser vivo necesita para vivir. Las plantas crecen cuando se satifacen sus **necesidades.**

nutrients (nü′ trē ənts) Materials that living things need. Plants need **nutrients** to change and grow.

nutrientes Sustancias que los seres vivos necesitan. Las plantas necesitan **nutrientes** para cambiar y crecer.

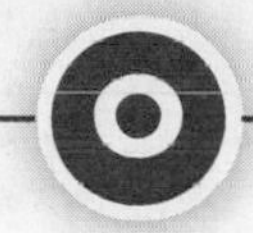

observe (əb sėrv′) When you use your senses. You can **observe** sounds that an animal makes.

observar Cuando usas tus sentidos. Puedes **observar** los sonidos que hace un animal.

ocean (ō′ shən) A large salty body of water. Some fish live in an **ocean** habitat.

océano Cuerpo grande de agua salada. El hábitat donde viven algunos peces es el **océano.**

record (ri kôrd′) When scientists write or draw what they learn. It is important to **record** information during experiments.

Favorite Animals					
cat					
dog					
bird					

registrar Cuando los científicos escriben o dibujan lo que descubren. Es importante **registrar** la información durante un experimento.

S

safety (sāf′ tē) Staying out of danger. The girl washes her hands to stay **safe.**

seguridad Estar fuera de peligro. La niña se lava las manos para mantenerse **segura.**

shelter (shel′ tər) A safe place. The beaver uses sticks and mud for **shelter.**

albergue Lugar seguro. El castor usa palitos y lodo para hacer su **albergue.**

soil (soil) The top layer of Earth. You can find rocks in **soil.**

suelo La capa superior de la Tierra. Puedes hallar rocas en el **suelo.**

solid (sol′ id) Matter that has its own size and shape. Each toy in the box is a **solid.**

sólido Materia que tiene forma y tamaño propios. Todos los juguetes de la caja son **sólidos.**

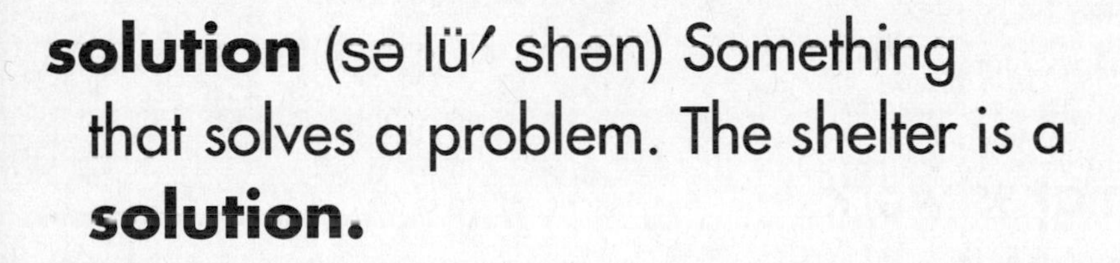

solution (sə lü′ shən) Something that solves a problem. The shelter is a **solution.**

solución Algo que resuelve un problema. El albergue es una **solución.**

T

technology (tek nol′ ə jē) Using science to help solve problems. A computer is **technology.**

tecnología Usar las ciencias para resolver problemas. Una computadora es **tecnología.**

terrarium (tə rar′ ē əm) A glass tank where plants and small animals live. Plants and small animals can live in a **terrarium.**

terrario Tanque de vidrio donde viven plantas y animales pequeños. Las plantas y los pequeños animales pueden vivir en un **terrario.**

tool (tül) Something that makes work easier. A hand lens is a **tool** that helps you see things.

instrumento Algo que te ayuda a hacer tu trabajo. Una lupa es un **instrumento** que te ayuda ver cosas.

W

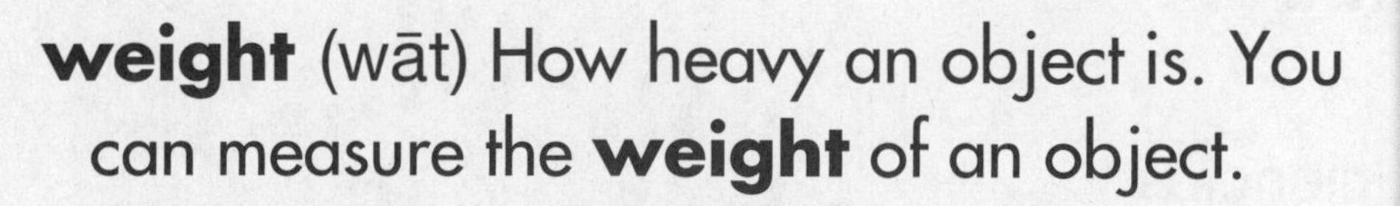

weight (wāt) How heavy an object is. You can measure the **weight** of an object.

peso Cuán pesado es un objeto. Puedes medir el **peso** de un objeto.

wetland (wet′ land′) Habitat that is covered in water. Tanya saw a blue heron when she visited the **wetland** near her home.

pantanal Hábitat cubierto de agua. Tanya vio una garza ceniza cuando fue al **pantanal** que queda cerca de su casa.

Index

This index lists the pages on which topics appear in this book. Page numbers after a *p* refer to a photograph. Page numbers following a *c* refer to a chart or graph.

D

M

P

Q

R

S

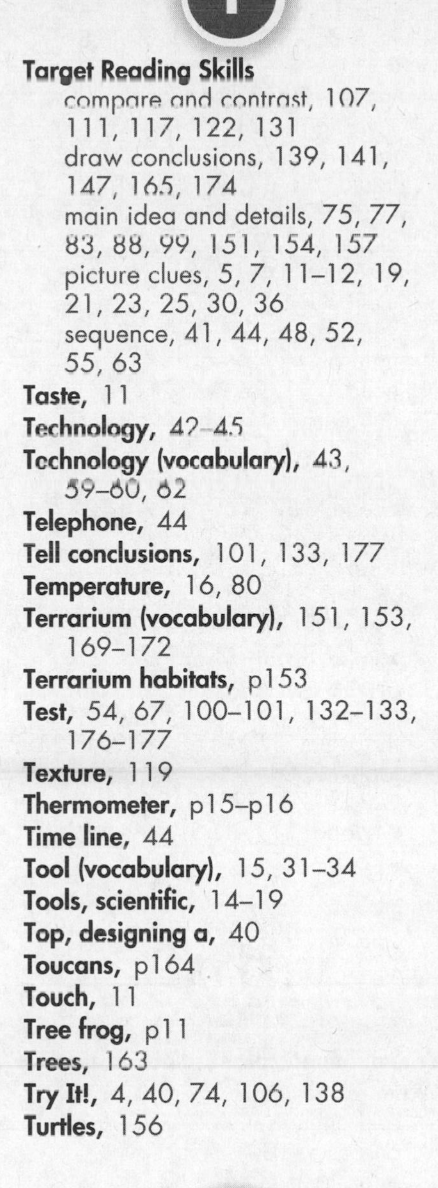

T

V

W

Credits

Staff Credits

The people who made up the *Interactive Science* team — representing composition services, core design digital and multimedia production services, digital product development, editorial, editorial services, manufacturing, and production — are listed below.

Geri Amani, Alisa Anderson, Jose Arrendondo, Amy Austin, Scott Baker, Lindsay Bellino, Charlie Bink, Bridget Binstock, Holly Blessen, Robin Bobo, Craig Bottomley, Jim Brady, Laura Brancky, Chris Budzisz, Mary Chingwa, Sitha Chhor, Caroline Chung, Margaret Clampitt, Kier Cline, Brandon Cole, Mitch Coulter, AnnMarie Coyne, Fran Curran, Dana Damiano, Nancy Duffner, Amanda Ferguson, David Gall, Mark Geyer, Amy Goodwin, Gerardine Griffin, Chris Haggerty, Laura Hancko, Jericho Hernandez, Autumn Hickenlooper, Guy Huff, George Jacobson, Marian Jones, Kathi Kalina, Chris Kammer, Sheila Kanitsch, Alyse Kondrat, Mary Kramer, Thea Limpus, Dominique Mariano, Lori McGuire, Melinda Medina, Angelina Mendez, Claudi Mimo, John Moore, Phoebe Novak, Anthony Nuccio, Jeffrey Osier, Julianne Regnier, Charlene Rimsa, Rebecca Roberts, Camille Salerno, Manuel Sanchez, Carol Schmitz, Amanda Seldera, Sheetal Shah, Jeannine Shelton El, Geri Shulman, Greg Sorenson, Samantha Sparkman, Mindy Spelius, Karen Stockwell, Dee Sunday, Dennis Tarwood, Jennie Teece, Lois Teesdale, Michaela Tudela, Oscar Vera, Dave Wade, Tom Wickland, James Yagelski, Tim Yetzina, Diane Zimmermann

Illustrations

1, 70, 72, 76, 127, 135, 152, 163 Precision Graphics
All other illustrations Chandler Digital Art

Photographs

Every effort has been made to secure permission and provide appropriate credit for photographic material. The publisher deeply regrets any omission and pledges to correct errors called to its attention in subsequent editions.

Unless otherwise acknowledged, all photographs are the property of Pearson Education, Inc.

Photo locators denoted as follows: Top (T), Center (C), Bottom (B), Left (L), Right (R), Background (Bkgd)

COVER: ©Davies and Starr/Getty Images

1 (TC) ©Corbis/Shutterstock; 2 ©Daniel Dempster Photography/Alamy, (C) Dave King/©DK Images; 5 (C) ©Corbis/Jupiter Images; 6 (TR) ©Corbis/Shutterstock, (Bkgd) Photos to Go/Photolibrary, (TR) Popperfoto/Getty Images; 7 (CR) ©Zefa/SuperStock; 8 (C) ©Victor Leonidovich/Shutterstock; 9 (TR) ©OJO Images Ltd/Alamy; 10 (TR) ©Robyn Mackenzie/Shutterstock; 11 (CR) Thinkstock; 12 (C) Carlos Davilla/Getty Images; 15 (BR) ©OJO Images Ltd./Alamy; 18 (B) ©Indeed/Getty Images; 20 (TR) ©Susan E. Degginger/Alamy Images; 21 (CR) ©Davis Barber/PhotoEdit, Inc.; 23 (CR) ©Getty Images/Jupiter Images; 24 (TR) ©Martin Ruegner/Getty Images; 25 (CR) ©Radius Images/Alamy; 26 (C, B) Jupiter Images; 27 (T, B) Jupiter Images; 30 (BR, BL) ©Goddard Space Flight Center/NASA; 31 (BL) ©Davis Barber/PhotoEdit, Inc., (CL) ©Indeed/Getty Images, (TR) ©Zefa/SuperStock, (CR) Thinkstock, 33 (TR) ©Radius Images/Alamy, 35 (BL) ©Martin Ruegner/Getty Images, (BC) ©Susan E. Degginger/Alamy Images, (T) ©Zefa/SuperStock, (B) Dave King/©DK Images, (TC) Thinkstock; 36 (B) ©TongRo Image Stock/Alamy, (CR, CL) Jupiter Images; 38 ©Lisette Le Bon/SuperStock; 41 Andy Crawford/©DK Images; 42 (TR) ©StijntS/Shutterstock; 43 (CR) Jupiter Images; 44 (BC) ©SSPL/Getty Images, (BL) DK Images, (CL) Jupiter Images, (BR) Reprinted with permission of Unisys Corporation; 45 (TR) ©Adam Gault/Getty Images; 46 (T) ©Derrick Alderman/Alamy Images, ©George Rose/Getty Images; 49 (TC) ©Hemera Technologies/Thinkstock, ©Jupiterimages/Thinkstock; 51 ©Masterfile Royalty-Free, ©Tom & Pat Leeson/Photo Researchers, Inc.; 52 ©Kim Karpeles/Alamy Images; 53 (BL) ©Comstock Images/Thinkstock, ©Comstock/Thinkstock, ©Jupiterimages/Thinkstock; 54 (T) ©Masterfile Royalty-Free, (C) ©Tim Platt/Getty Images; 58 ©JHP Signs/Alamy Images; 59 (TL) ©Tom & Pat Leeson/Photo Researchers, Inc., (TR) Jupiter Images; 61 (C) ©Derrick Alderman/Alamy Images, (T) ©Kim Karpeles/Alamy Images; 62 (BR) ©David Davis/Shutterstock, (BC) Getty Images; 64 (C) ©Kari Marttila/Alamy; 74 (TR) ©JG Photography/Alamy; 78 (T) Shutterstock; 84 (B) ©Kari Marttila/Alamy, (R) ©SCPhotos/Alamy; 89 (TC) ©JG Photography/Alamy; 91 Stockdisc; 96 Shutterstock; 99 (C) ©amygdala imagery/Shutterstock, (T) ©Rob Byron/Shutterstock; 100 (CR) ©Wolfgang Kaehler/Corbis, (TR) Photos to Go/Photolibrary; 102 (TR) ©Danita Delimont/Alamy Images, (Bkgd) ©gary718/Shutterstock, (CR, BR) Jupiter Images; 104 (C) ©J. Jangoux/Photo Researchers, Inc., (CL) ©Kevin Eaves/Shutterstock, (Bkgd) Lisa Walston, (CR) Thinkstock; 106 (T) ©Clearviewstock/Alamy; 107 (CR) ©Hugh Threlfall/Alamy Images; 110 (TR, TC) Colin Keates/Courtesy of the Natural History Museum, London/©DK Images; 111 (TR) Jupiter Images, (BR) Matthew Ward/Peter Griffiths - modelmaker/©DK Images, (TL) Paul Bricknell/©DK Images; 112 (BR) Clive Streeter/DK Images, (BL) Peter Anderson/©DK Images; 113 (T) ©DK Images; 114 (B) ©Witold Skrypczak/Alamy, (T) Andy Crawford/©DK Images; 115 (C) ©DK Images, (TL) Andy Crawford/©DK Images, (TR) Photolibrary Group, Inc.; 118 (Bkgd) ©Getty Images/Jupiter Images; 121 (BL) Clive Streeter/DK Images, (T) Photos to Go/Photolibrary, (B) Shutterstock; 122 ©blickwinkel/Alamy Images, ©image100/Jupiter Images, (BR) ©Jan Wlodarczyk/Alamy Images; 128 (C) ©photosbyjohn/Shutterstock; 131 (T) ©Michael Patrick O'Neill/Alamy Images; 132 (T Bkgd) ©mycola/Shutterstock, (TL) ©Rannev/Shutterstock; 133 (TL) ©Galyna Andrushko/Shutterstock, (CR) Corbis; 134 ©Tony Sweet/Getty Images; 136 (TC) ©David Davis/Shutterstock, (CR) ©Jim Lopes/Shutterstock, (TL) ©Stefan Sollfors/Alamy; 137 (CR) ©Corbis/SuperStock, (TC) ©William Leaman/Alamy Images; 138 (C) ©imagebroker/Alamy Images; 140 ©Fernando Felix/Getty Images, (CR) ©Photodisc/SuperStock; 142 (T) ©Visions of America, LLC/Alamy, (T) Jupiter Images; 143 (CR) ©Lisa Dearing/Alamy; 144 (CR) ©Jerry Whaley/Alamy, (T) ©Lisa Dearing/Alamy; 145 (Bkgd) ©American Images Inc./Getty

Images, (BR) Dave King/©DK Images; 146 (Bkgd) ©Richard Broadwell/Alamy, (BR) Acorn Studios plc, London/©DK Images; 147 (BC) ©Daniel Sweeney (escapeimages)/Alamy, (CR) ©Steve Hamblin/Alamy; 148 (T) ©Masterfile Royalty-Free; 149 (CR) ©Vibe Images/Alamy; 150 ©FloridaStock/Shutterstock; 151 (B) Jupiter Images; 153 (TR) ©Ingram Publishing/Jupiter Images; 154 (T) ©imagebroker/Alamy Images; 155 ©David Sieren/Getty Images, (CL) ©Martin Ruegner/Getty Images, ©Picavet/Getty Images; 156 ©Nancy Nehring/Getty Images, ©Rebecca Yale/Getty Images, ©Rob Blakers/Getty Images, Ryu Uchiyama/Minden Pictures; 157 ©Duane Rieder/Getty Images, ©Image Source , ©Martha Catherine Ivey/Getty Images, ©Medioimages/Photodisc/Getty Images, ©Wolfgang Bayer/Getty Images; 160 ©Cathy Melloan/PhotoEdit, Inc., ©Danita Delimont/Alamy Images; 161 (C) ©imagebroker/Alamy Images, (TL, CL) ©Lisa Dearing/Alamy, (CR) ©Tony Sweet/Getty Images; 163 (BL) ©FloridaStock/Shutterstock, (TR) ©Richard Broadwell/Alamy; 165 (CL) ©Lisa Dearing/Alamy, (BC) ©Masterfile Royalty-Free, (TL) ©mycola/Shutterstock, (C) ©photosbyjohn/Shutterstock, (CL) ©William Leaman/Alamy Images; 166 (C) Digital Vision; 167 (TL) ©fotoandrea/Shutterstock, (TR) ©Razvan Chirnoaga/Shutterstock, (TC) Jupiter Images; X001 ©Daniel Dempster Photography/Alamy; X002 (T) ©niderlander/Shutterstock; X003 (BL) ©James Thew/Shutterstock.

This space is yours. Draw pictures and write words.

This is your book.

You can write in it.

interactive
SCIENCE

This is your book.

You can write in it.

interactive
SCIENCE

This is your book.

You can write in it.